Murder

Goes

Jazz

Book 10

A Dodo Dorchester
Mystery

By

Ann Sutton

The hottest American jazz band, fresh from New Orleans. A clandestine party full of 'bright young things' in the middle of London's East End. When murder kills the celebration, will Dodo catch the culprit before Scotland Yard? Or will she be the next victim?

When a legendary New Orleans jazz band arrives on Britain's balmy shores to play at a clandestine jazz party in a deserted warehouse, Dodo is more than excited. But the jubilant atmosphere takes a dark turn when a shocking murder occurs right under her nose.

With her keen mind and charming demeanor, Dodo dives into the case, navigating through a labyrinth of clues, motives, and potential suspects. As the tide of suspicion ebbs and flows, Dodo must navigate the fascinating and cut-throat world of jazz before the killer strikes a haunting final chord.

Close the blinds, grab your favorite drink, and curl up with this fun, suspenseful Golden Age cozy mystery today!

Published by

Wild Poppy Publishing LLC
Highland, UT 84003

Distributed by Wild Poppy Publishing

Cover design by Julie Matern
Cover Design ©2023 Wild Poppy Publishing LLC

Edited by Waypoint Authors

Dedicated to James Sutton

Style Note

I am a naturalized American citizen born and raised in the United Kingdom. I have readers in America, the UK, Australia, Canada and beyond. But my book is set in the United Kingdom.

So which version of English should I choose?

I chose American English as it is my biggest audience, my family learns this English and my editor suggested it was the most logical.

This leads to criticism from those in other English-speaking countries, but I have neither the time nor the resources to do a special edition for each country.

I do use British words, phrases and idioms whenever I can (unless my editor does not understand them and then it behooves me to change it so that it is not confusing to my readers).

Titles and courtesy titles of the British nobility are complicated and somewhat dynamic through the ages. Earls, dukes and marquises have titles that are different from their family names. After extensive study on honorary titles and manners of address I have concluded that to the average reader it is all rather confusing and complicated. Earls, dukes and marquises have titles that are different from their family names which would be hard for readers to follow.

Therefore, in an attempt to eliminate this confusion, I have made the editorial decision to call Dodo's father Lord Dorchester rather than Lord Trent and her mother Lady Guinevere rather than Lady Trent.

Murder Goes Jazz Cast of Characters

Dorchester Family

Dorothea 'Dodo' Dorchester	Amateur sleuth and fashion ambassador
Diantha 'Didi" Dorchester	Dodo's sister
Lady Guinevere Dorchester	Dodo's mother
Lord Alfred Dorchester	Dodo's father
Lizzie	Dodo's maid
Ernest Scott	Lizzie's fiancée and Rupert's valet
Rupert Danforth	Dodo's boyfriend

Smokey Syncopation – Jazz Band

Lucille 'Lulu' Bassett	Lead singer
Cy Preston	Trumpet player
Lonnie Chapman	Pianist
Dex Dolby	Saxophone player

Crazy Train – Jazz Band

Miranda Masters	Lead singer
Gerry Waters	Drummer
Fred Garrett	Pianist

David Bellamy   Dodo's
                                 friend

Lady Harriet Plumford   David's
                                 friend

Table of Contents

Chapter 1

Dressed in sophisticated black from head to toe, Renée Dubois' scarlet lips pinched tight around the silver pins as her nimble fingers pulled and tucked the ivory, pearl satin around Diantha Dorchester's slim frame. Dodo's heart was beating rapidly but not because of a gruesome murder. This time, her heart was overflowing with happiness as the bespoke wedding dress came to life on her little sister. *Stunning!*

Cloistered in her sister's feminine boudoir, Dodo examined the French fashion sketch in her hand and compared it to the gown coming to life before her. This wedding dress was going to be unlike any other in the world, but Dodo was confident it would catch on as soon as it made an appearance in the society rags—which it was certain to do.

The smooth satin formed a custom, body-hugging shift which would sit under an exquisite handmade Breton lace gown with a cathedral train. The sketch also showcased a unique bandeau with clusters of delicate, satin roses on each side which anchored an exceptionally long veil of the same Breton lace.

"I can begin to see it," whispered Lady Guinevere, her eyes shining as she beheld her youngest daughter. "You will look like an angel, darling. Absolutely breathtaking!"

Renée, the famous designer, pushed up from kneeling on the floor. As the head of a thriving fashion house, she rarely had hands on any projects these days, but since Dodo Dorchester was her most valued fashion ambassador as well as a personal friend, she had insisted on handmaking Didi's dress herself.

"You should be one of my models," said Renée in impeccable English. "It is a pleasure to work with such a divine figure." The honor of the suggestion was not lost on Dodo, but it was out of the question.

Didi's cheeks lit up like the magnificent wild poppies that bloomed annually on the Dorchester estate. Unlike her sister, Didi was unused to being in the limelight.

Dodo replaced the sketch on the side table, glancing at her traditional mother. "Didi is far too busy getting ready for her wedding for such fancies." Plus, Lady Guinevere Dorchester would *never* permit the daughter of an earl to do anything as risqué as prance about on a public catwalk for strangers to ogle.

"It's terribly nice to receive the compliment though," said Didi, the flush of embarrassment settling into a pinkish hue on her milky skin as she looked over her shoulder into the long mirror.

"No doubt!" agreed Dodo.

Arms akimbo, Renée watched Didi's movement with experienced eyes. "You can move well, yes?"

"I shall have no problem performing the *Black Bottom* if that's what you mean," said Didi, shimmying her graceful hips in demonstration.

"Génial!" declared Renée. "Casting off those old-fashioned corsets and stiff Edwardian dresses has liberated women in more ways than one, no?"

Dodo peeked across the room at her mother who still wore her corsets for social occasions to nip and narrow her middle-aged figure. Lady Dorchester was pursing her lips, a telltale sign that she was biting back a comment.

"I don't know why Granny insists on still wearing hers every day," added Didi, still admiring the snug shift from every direction.

"Because she believes her body will fall apart if it is not stuffed into a tight prison," declared Dodo, adding a dose of humor to the situation. "And at her age, she may be right!"

2

They all fell about laughing.

"That will do for today," said Renée, helping Didi out of the heavenly gown. "May I return in, say, three days?"

"That should be fine," said Didi. "Charlie is swatting hard for his final exams, so I have plenty of extra time on my hands at the moment." Charlie Chadwick, Didi's fiancé, was an old friend of the family and a current graduate student, aiming to become a history professor. He and Didi were to be married two weeks after his final exams.

"Can you stay for dinner?" Dodo's mother asked Renée.

"Oh, Lady Dorchester! You are too kind! Though I thank you for the invitation, I cannot." She wiggled her brows beneath a boyishly short haircut. "I have a previous engagement. I am here, in England, with my husband who has a business dinner this evening in town." Renée had married her financial backer just over a year ago in a short ceremony at the *marie*, or French courthouse. Dodo had been the maid of honor at the simple, private affair.

"Oh, I'd love to see him!" declared Dodo. "Perhaps you can fit in a dinner with Rupert and I while you are here?"

Renée looked up from placing the tools of her trade into a large, cow-hide bag. "I should like very much to meet this Rupert I have heard so much about. How about Thursday?"

"I'll have to check with him, but I know I'm free."

"We're staying at the Radford in Mayfair. You can leave a message." She snapped the eye-catching, black-and-white bag shut. "Now, I must dash." She leaned in to give both the girls and their mother the French *bises*, or kisses on the cheek. "Au revoir!"

With a flick of her delicate wrist, Renée flounced out of Didi's bedroom and down the sweeping staircase.

"Wow! What a force of nature that woman is!" declared Lady Guinevere. "Though she looks like she has just come from a funeral dressed all in black like that, I must admit the French seem to have a certain innate grace that we British must learn."

3

"I agree," said Dodo. "They sling a scarf around their neck as they head out the door and it seems like they just walked off a Parisian catwalk while we British struggle with the blessed scarf for ages only for it to look like an awkward addition."

"Not when *you* do it," retorted Didi, securing a silk wrap around her thin waist.

"That's because I've spent a lot of time practicing," Dodo admitted. "Any French schoolgirl seems to achieve the same elegant look effortlessly."

"Well, be that as it may, thoroughly English Didi will steal the show in that magical wedding dress," sighed Lady Guinevere. "Renée certainly possesses an undeniable genius for design."

"She does," agreed Dodo. "Not only that, but she's also endowed with an innate business acumen, which means she's intelligent enough to employ others with similar talent to work for her."

"Let's not forget about the English Lady who offers her opinions on the designs too," added her mother, referring to Dodo's association with the designer.

Dodo rolled her eyes with a coy smile. "I play a small part. In fact, I picked out this design for Didi from several others. I immediately knew this was the one. Even Princess Mary will be green with envy."

"I agree!" said her mother, laughing with a twinkle in her eye.

With plans to meet her boyfriend, Rupert Danforth, at the Lyceum Theater for a showing of *Midsummer Night's Dream*, Dodo had dressed to kill. It never hurt to remind one's beau why he fell for you.

Rupert was waiting for her at the bottom of the steps and hadn't spotted Dodo yet. More than one woman took a

4

second look as they passed him. His face lit up when his eyes found Dodo's.

"Woah!" He held her at arm's length, sweeping appreciative eyes over her gown, then pulling her close and kissing her on the cheek. "Just when I think you can't get any more beautiful, you prove me wrong."

Dressed in a dinner jacket and neat, white bowtie, her heart skipped at the sight of him. "Likewise!"

Taking her hand, they entered the Greek revival building and stepped into the opulent lobby which encircled patrons in a delightful hug of warm oak. Anything that wasn't wrapped in the English wood was a deep, rich burgundy.

"Do you fancy a cocktail before we find our seats?" Rupert asked, checking his chunky watch.

"I do rather," Dodo replied as they made for the bar which simply dripped with crystal chandeliers.

Planting a shoe on the shiny, brass footrest, Rupert ordered their favorite drinks. Dodo situated her back against the polished wood, resting her elbows on the bar and surveying those who entered. Most women were thoroughly modern with only the odd holdout.

"Here you go," said the bartender, handing her the wide-mouthed glass. She took a small sip, letting the cool liquid pleasantly burn as her eye caught a flash of familiar blond hair.

"David!" she cried.

Rupert pivoted as David Bellamy, Dodo's old friend and bottomless library of society gossip, pushed his way through the fashionable crowd.

"Darlings!" he cried, rushing forward with open arms, a petite, plain-faced female in his wake.

He smothered Dodo in European kisses as the vacant looking girl looked on, then grabbed Rupert by the shoulder, pumping his hand. "What a lovely surprise!"

Even for David, this was an energetic greeting. Dodo tipped her head toward the flapper.

David's face fell three stories. "Oh, yes! Allow me to introduce Lady Harriet Plumford."

Instead of the introduction animating the insipid girl's dull features, she blinked like a barn owl in fancy dress. David nudged her.

Sounding like a dormouse on death's door, she managed, "How do you do?"

Dodo locked eyes with David, a question on her brow. She was as unlike his usual companions as it was possible to be.

"Harriet is the sister of an old school chum. She is down here for the tennis with her mother. My friend asked me to show his sister around. She's from Darby."

Now things were starting to make more sense. David was more a music hall attendee than a Shakespearean enthusiast.

"Can I get you both a drink?" Rupert asked.

"A Corpse Reviver for me, if you don't mind?" said David. "How about you, Harriet?"

"Uh. What? Oh! A gin and tonic, please." Rupert had to lean in to hear her small voice.

After he placed the order, David grinned, rubbing his hands together. "When's the next SJP?" He was referring to the "Secret Jazz Parties", so named by attendees, that Rupert organized periodically around the city's capital.

Rupert's head snapped from side to side. "Steady on, old chap! Remember, I'm anonymous. Don't want anyone to know."

David's features dropped into a knowing smile as he tapped his nose. "Your secret's safe with me." He leaned in closer. "Well?"

"I'm finishing up the details of one for next week, as it happens."

"I haven't heard a thing," gasped David, clutching his chest.

"Perhaps you're not as notorious as you think you are," said Dodo with a side of snide.

David pulled on his jacket lapels. "We all know that's not it, darling."

The SJPs were not advertised in the usual way. It was all done by word of mouth. Rupert would put out a rumor in a carefully selected group and then let the magic happen. Dodo had not yet been to one of his parties and was terrifically excited.

Rupert took a sip and spoke quietly into his glass. "It may be at the large, abandoned warehouse in Millward Yard on the Isle of Dogs at eleven, Friday next."

"Ooh! Can I help spread the rumor?" asked David like a schoolboy hearing about a lemon drop sale.

"As long as you don't mention me, of course," replied Rupert with a grin. "The more the merrier."

The lights in the foyer dimmed, indicating that it was time to find their seats.

"Let's meet up again at the interval," suggested David. Touching Dodo's head with his own, he whispered, "I may need some jolly company by then."

As Rupert and Dodo descended the stairs at the intermission, a high-pitched shriek of laughter caught their attention. Glancing back, the crowd was too thick to see who it was. Elegant people swarmed the foyer like ants chasing a crumb of cake.

"Grab a table and I'll get you another drink," said Rupert.

"No cocktail this time, sweetheart. Remember, I only have one a night. Pineapple juice will suit me fine."

They parted company and Dodo slithered through the crowd at the bar to snag a table. She managed to seize one just before another woman was about to claim it.

"Look, there's another," she said helpfully, pointing out another table.

The vulgar shriek of laughter split the air again, only louder this time, and Dodo spotted David, frantic like a mother at her wits end with a naughty child. Behind him, appeared the caterwauling culprit.

Lady Harriet Plumford!

Eyes willing Dodo to kill him, David gasped, "Apparently, Harriet can't take her liquor. She's like Jekyll and Hyde. Chattering non-stop during the play and hands all over me. I'm going to kill her brother."

By this time, the more-than-slightly inebriated Harriet had caught up.

"What a jolly show!" Harriet wailed, laughing hysterically. "I just love those fairies!"

Though *A Midsummer Night's Dream* was one of the Bard's more light-hearted works, it could hardly be described as hilarious.

Harriet bounced into a chair, eyes alert, scanning the crowd. "Why don't you get me another drink, David darling?"

"I think you've had quite enough for one evening," declared David, sitting across the table as far from her as humanly possible.

"But I'm just getting started," she pouted, cheeks aflame.

"I'm having pineapple juice," said Dodo. "How about some of that instead?"

Harriet wrinkled her nose. "Can you put gin in it?"

Dodo winked at David. "Of course. Off you go, David!"

"It's good to see someone enjoying a classic so much," Dodo said once David was gone on his commission.

Harriet flung her arms back, and in a voice several decibels too loud, declared, "Oh, I don't really like old Shakey, but Mummy insisted we see something respectable."

8

Several pairs of judgmental eyes were shooting darts in their direction.

"What *do* you like?" asked Dodo, hoping to quell her fervor.

"Jazz. Dancing. Cocktails," sang Harriet just as Rupert returned with hands full of glasses.

Dodo raised her brows at him. "Harriet's gin and tonic loosened her up a little."

"I can hear that," agreed Rupert.

"I was just telling Dolly here I'd rather be dancing to jazz in a club," howled Harriet.

"It's Dodo," Rupert corrected.

"Dodo, Dolly, Dotty. What's the diff?" Harriet began cackling just like a witch in another of the Bard's plays.

"Do you go to clubs often?" Rupert asked, his mouth hitching up on one side.

Harriet flapped both arms wildly. "Never! Mother won't let me. But I dream about it."

Dodo was fast building a picture of an oppressed young woman who hid a wild side that escaped when fueled with alcohol.

"What is *your* favorite club?" Harriet asked, making eyes at Rupert.

Dodo had to purse her lips to stop from smiling, but her eyes were giving her away.

"I like variety," he responded vaguely. "Don't like sticking to one spot."

Harriet squinted her eyes as if she and Rupert were planning some clandestine date. "I've heard the 43 Club is good."

"Depends what you mean by *good*," Dodo added. "Good if you want to ruin your reputation."

This was the wrong thing to say and set the girl off sounding like a hyena again. Their table had become quite the carnival attraction.

"Here," said David, placing two glasses on the table. "One pineapple juice…and gin."

Harriet picked up the glass and slung the contents down her throat like a dock worker.

Thank goodness it was virtuous as a nun.

Dodo took a sip of her own, keeping an eye on Harriet.

"Harriet was just telling us she has a penchant for questionable jazz clubs," said Rupert, slapping David on the back.

If Rupert had just told David he had been conscripted onto a naval ship he could not have looked more hopeless. "Is that so? Well, she'll have to find another person to take her there. Far too risqué for me."

Now Dodo wanted to laugh.

The lights dimmed. "Time for the second act," announced Dodo.

"Wish me luck!" replied David, urgency lacing every word.

Chapter 2

Shadows of tall, brick warehouses formed the impression of a West End, cityscape backdrop of some avant-garde play. Dodo and Didi had chattered with pent up excitement all the way to town, but now, as they peered out the windows of the car into the dark gloom of the deserted building, their conversation dried up.

"Are you sure this is it, m'lady?" asked their chauffeur. "Looks abandoned to me."

They had arrived earlier than was fashionable because Rupert was running the party, which meant that no other partygoers could be seen. Dodo withdrew the note with the address from her clutch bag.

"Building 5, West Ferry Road."

"Well, this *is* West Ferry Road,' the chauffeur replied. "But it's not like the buildings have letters—wait, they do. Look! It's faded and hard to see in the dark, but it does look like a five."

As the girls hesitated, a van with "Savoy" written on the side crawled past.

"This is it!" cried Dodo in triumph. "That's who provides the food and drink."

The chauffeur stopped the car and walked around to open the door. Dodo noticed he was wrinkling his nose, and as she stepped out, the smell of fish and sewage hit her senses.

She coughed.

"This building might be deserted, but the rest of the place is a working dock in the daytime," explained the chauffeur.

"Indeed." She withdrew a scented handkerchief from her clutch.

11

"Woah!" cried Didi, sliding out behind her. "What a fishy stink."

"When will you need me, m'lady?" asked the driver.

"I shouldn't think before four in the morning. Do you have somewhere to go?"

"Don't you worry about me, m'lady. I have an aunty who lives close by. I'm going to have a kip round there."

"Splendid!"

A gust of wind draped them with a stronger stench like an invisible cape, and she and Didi ran in the direction of the Savoy van down a dark alley.

The only light was from the half-moon playing hide and seek behind the clouds. *Splash!* A puddle! It soaked through her silk stocking.

"Uggh!" cried Didi as her foot did the same.

The alley narrowed and Dodo ignored the squeaks of vermin complaining as she flashed by in search of some kind of service entrance.

A side door, camouflaged by the wall, suddenly opened, and Dodo almost smashed into it in her haste but instead landed in the arms of Rupert. Didi was hot on her heels and bumped into them both, knocking the pair into a towering, muscular, bald fellow dressed in black.

"Who's this then?" he asked in a surprisingly baritone, thick, cockney accent.

"These are VIPs," Rupert assured him. "They have a *special* invitation and are permitted to use this door, unlike the other partygoers."

The giant, bald man looked them both up and down with appreciation. "If you say so, guv!"

"That was quite an entrance!" Rupert chuckled, as the beefy chap headed in another direction. "You found the place alright?"

Dodo smoothed her dress while her heart beat an adrenaline-fueled tattoo. "You weren't kidding when you said you choose seedy places for these bashes. There may be more rats around here than 'bright young things'."

Rupert put a hand to his chest, a dramatic expression of pain on his fine features. "You have cut me to the quick, darling!" Then his features melted into that heart-stopping smile. "Keeps the riff-raff away."

He directed the caterer to the inside and took Dodo's hand while Didi followed. Inside was a cavernous space. Temporary lights on stands were placed at intervals around the room and a group of musicians were getting their equipment ready on a raised dais. As for decorations, there were very few, but Rupert had repeated a trick he created for her twenty-first birthday party—a light with a photograph film attached to the front that projected huge images onto the walls.

"What do you think?" he asked, looking more vulnerable than Dodo expected.

"It's fabulous!" she responded. "Creepy yet thrilling. I can see why these things are so popular." A pleasant breeze brushed her bare shoulders, and she looked up to see high, open windows. "Shame about the smell."

"Your nose will get used to it in a bit," he assured her with a wry grin.

"It's super, Rupert!" declared Didi, eyes shining with excitement. "I totally understand why people come—it's just a little bit dangerous. Heightens the illicit atmosphere."

Rupert's shoulders relaxed. "That's what they tell me." He glanced at his watch. "People will begin arriving in about half an hour. Let me show you to my secret hideout."

He began to walk behind the small stage as the lead singer sang into the microphone. Dodo's head snapped around. *Lucille Bassett!* She would know that voice anywhere. She sang with Smokey Syncopation, a jazz band from America that were racing to the top of the popularity polls in England. How on earth did Rupert know them?

She tottered over to him on daringly high heels. "*Smokey Syncopation?*"

His eyes shone. "I didn't tell you because I wanted it to be a surprise."

"Well, you succeeded," she said. "You keep surprising me."

"Would you like to meet them?"

"Would I…?"

"I'll take that as an affirmative."

They spun round and Rupert led Dodo and her sister up onto the dais.

Lucille Basset was a full-figured beauty, her dark, hypnotic eyes full of mischief.

"Miss Bassett, I'd like to introduce you to my girl, Dodo."

Lucille's finely plucked brows pinched her bronzed skin. "What kind of a dumb name is that?" The cadence of her speech was just like the timbre of her singing—deep, rich and gravelly.

Dodo burst out laughing. She liked Lucille immediately and reached out a hand. "It's short for Dorothea. It's a pleasure to meet you, Miss Bassett."

Lucille took her hand in a firm shake, and through full, scarlet lips said, "Oh please, you can call me Lucille or Lulu. I didn't offend you, did I?" The end of her sentence trailed up in the pleasant resonance of the Deep South.

"Not in the least," Dodo assured her.

"Then how d'ya do?" Lucille's charming smile rolled around her face as she cast an eye over Dodo's glamorous, silver gown. "That is some get-up, toots."

"Thank you," said Dodo, running fingers down the sequins that caught the dim lighting and sparkled.

A squeak from beside reminded Dodo that Didi's silence meant she was starstruck.

"Allow me to introduce my sister, Didi. Short for Diantha. We're both huge fans of yours Miss—Lulu."

14

Didi looked like she might explode with excitement and merely giggled.

"Cy! Dex! Lonnie! Get over here and meet these fine ladies." There was no doubt who was in charge of the band as the aging pianist, trumpet and saxophone players lumbered over.

"Mighty fine to meet you," gushed the pianist, doffing his trilby with a smile bigger than Georgia. "Name's Lonnie." Dodo and Didi shook his hand as he cast a respectful but appreciative eye over the pair of them.

"Evenin'," said a tall, younger man, a saxophone hanging from a cord around his neck, in a deep, rumbling voice that rippled over Dodo's skin. "Dex at your service." He touched a finger to his forehead but did not extend his hand.

"A pleasure! Cy Preston." The heavyset band member reached out a hand while the other held a shiny, brass trumpet. Cy had a distinctive scar that ran past his left eye, crinkling the otherwise smooth, dark skin. In a deserted alley he might look menacing, but a captivating smile disarmed Dodo completely. His ebony eyes were full of untold stories as they searched hers, and his strong hand felt rough.

"We'll let you rehearse," suggested Rupert, and though Dodo knew he was right, she had to drag herself away from the rising stars whose rhythmic music stirred her soul.

Didi found her voice at last. "Rupert! How did you manage it?"

Rupert dropped his eyes, the vision of humility. "They approached me, actually. This is their first trip across the pond. They're booked to play in several cities, including London, and my little soirée came to their attention."

Dodo gestured with her arm. "These are hardly little, Rupert, but I am impressed by your modesty."

Rupert led them behind the stage to a narrow door camouflaged by a dark curtain. Opening it with a large key, he took Dodo and her sister into a square, sparse room housing several chairs, and a rickety table holding wine bottles and glasses and some fancy canapés.

"This is called the Green Room. It's where I begin the evening," he explained taking one of the chairs. "After about an hour, I sneak out and join the dancing throngs."

Dodo shook her head. "What an empire you've created."

"It didn't start out that way," he explained. "A couple of pals and I thought it would be fun to host an underground party for our friends. I took the lead and found a cheap venue, an unknown jazz band and provided some drinks and simple food. We didn't do formal invites, just told a few classmates and acquaintances the time and place and asked a small cover charge. We had room for maybe fifty. Three hundred people showed up! I realized there was demand for such a thing, and chatter confirmed that rather than put people off, the grungy location was a hit. That's when I decided to broaden my sights and make it into a business."

"And the attendees still don't know you're behind it all?" asked Dodo.

"No! The two friends who organized the first one with me got married and moved, one to Scotland and one to Australia. That first party on my own, I experienced a lot of growing pains and was constantly putting out fires behind the scenes. I never actually made it to the party. By the end, I was physically and emotionally exhausted and fell asleep in a back room around dawn. By the time I awoke, the sun was up and the building empty. When I emerged, I felt like the sole man on the moon. I thought the whole thing had been a grand failure, but in the weeks that followed, I heard rumors about it, and this great mythical fable began to evolve around the event. I just listened. People were enthralled that the host was some mystical, shadowy figure which unwittingly gave more credence to the whole enterprise.

16

"I decided to run with it and make that aspect of the events an integral part of the whole experience. I use third party contacts, different people every time, to make all the arrangements. That way my fingerprints aren't on anything. Then I show up on the night like some orchestra conductor, hours before the event, and hide out in a secret room until I think it's safe to mingle."

"The band knows it is you, though, surely?" said Didi.

Rupert scrunched that perfect nose. "Well, yes and no. They know I'm a cog in the wheel, but even they don't know I'm the brains behind the whole thing. And anyway, we make them sign a contract of non-disclosure. They're paid handsomely from the cover charges, and if they let the cat out of the bag in any way, they will never be invited back. So far it has worked out beautifully."

"Does your family know?" asked Dodo, thinking of Rupert's conservative parents she had met at Christmas.

"No one knows. Not even my sisters. I like to keep the whole thing…separate."

"No one?" she asked, incredulously.

"Well, now you and Didi…and my accountant. That's it."

"I feel privileged," said Dodo with a smile.

"So you should. Now, relax in here and I will ensure everything is running like clockwork." He retrieved a clip board and pencil and made for the door, then turned his head. "It's rather funny, actually. I hold the clipboard and keep talking about the 'boss'. Like I'm just some schlump on the payroll, and because I use different people to do the grunt work every time, no one catches on."

"He's good," said Didi, reaching for a caviar canapé after the door to the Green Room closed.

Dodo twisted her mouth. "He's better than good. Even David didn't know Rupert was behind these things."

"That *is* an accomplishment," agreed Didi.

"I suppose that's one more person who knows, but he was sworn to secrecy. David likes holding cards no one else does, so I don't think he will ever let it slip. He's coming to his first one tonight and is as excited as a child."

The sultry strains of a sad saxophone drifted through the walls, and Dodo leaned back in her chair, drinking it in. The Green Room was lit by one small lamp that cast dusty shadows around the walls. Not glamorous by any stretch of the imagination, but the secrecy leant itself to an anticipation she had not felt since she was a young girl. She was beginning to understand why the SJPs were so popular. The piano joined in on the other side of the wall and the lilting voice of Lucille Bassett crept through the walls and deep into Dodo's marrow. She closed her eyes.

Didi went to the door and opened it a crack, pushing the curtain aside. "I can see several hulking men dressed in black having a conflab in the middle of the room."

"I bet they are the bouncers," murmured Dodo. "Just like the one who stopped us at the door."

"Um, yes. Oh, and now there are a few young waiters standing at a makeshift bar and behind the food tables."

The jazzy music changed beat as it adjusted key, and Dodo felt the pleasant thump jump through her bloodstream. She checked her watch. Half-past eleven. She had been told the party really got going at midnight.

"Come back," she urged Didi. "I wouldn't want anyone to discover this room because of us."

Didi obliged and grabbed another canapé. "I'm so excited I can hardly eat!" By any standard Didi was a pretty girl, but the thrill of the upcoming event had heightened her appearance. It was a good thing an enormous diamond flashed on her left hand.

"Me too," agreed Dodo. "I'm not used to feeling this way at my age. It is rather exciting."

Didi opened a bottle of white wine. "I'm hoping Rupert can snag a popular band for my wedding reception."

18

"He managed it for my birthday party. He's a bit of a whizz in that department. Are you still going to have the reception outside?"

"Yes. Lots of white pavilion tents of course, in case it rains, but nothing is lovelier than Beresford House in the summer."

"I totally agree—"

Rupert slipped in, stopping her mid-sentence. "Everything is ready. I find this part rather addicting, actually. People are beginning to arrive." The color in his cheeks and the frantic spark in his eyes was a state Dodo was not used to seeing. Pride for his accomplishment blossomed in her chest like a drop of ink in water.

Chapter 3

Dodo could not eat anything. It felt like waiting for someone to have a baby. Rupert was relaxed, back against the chair, legs splayed in front of him. The band were playing some of their most famous numbers and her toes were tapping. The hum of partygoers penetrated the walls of the room as the building filled with young people eager for entertainment.

"Who knows you're back here?" she asked, to give her mouth something to do.

"Only Smokey Syncopation, the backup band, who have just arrived, and the head security fellow and the head waiter. The American band will come here between sets. The backup band, only after they have performed."

"Who are the other group?" she asked.

"A local, up-and-coming outfit. Gives them the all-important exposure and gives the main talent a break."

"And who finds them?"

He smirked. "Again, they come to me through the grapevine. It really is a well-oiled machine at this point."

"When can we go out there and dance," asked Didi. "My feet are more than ready."

"I'd say in another fifteen minutes. We'll file out one at a time to ensure we don't draw attention."

"It's so thrilling! It feels like we're doing something illegal when we're not."

Rupert ran a finger across his brow. "That is the wizardry. I have permits and bouncers and everything done legally but it feels shady."

"It's the environment as much as anything. That element of danger," said Dodo.

Snapping his fingers, Rupert said, "Exactly. And fortunately for me there are an unlimited number of such venues in London, so I shan't run out of them any time soon."

"I wish Charlie could have come with me," sighed Didi. "But he's having to make up for lost time since he took me to visit his family."

They talked about Charlie's plans for a while and the upcoming nuptials, then Rupert said, "Right, who wants to head out first?"

"Me!" cried Dodo, dying from anticipation.

"Alright. I'll send Didi out a few minutes after you and then I'll make an appearance."

Dodo quickly stuffed her clutch in a corner of the Green Room. Opening the door a fraction, she could see that the large warehouse was more than half filled with energetic dancers. The band was playing their latest tune, and everyone was making the most of it. She slipped out and shouldered her way through the crowd so she was not right next to the hidden door.

"Dodo!" *David.* "Where did you appear from?"

"I'm making my way around the room to see if I know anyone. And now I've found you." Rupert had asked her to keep the private room confidential, even from David.

"Where's your adorable sister?"

"Around somewhere." Dodo pretended to crane her neck to look for Didi, and as she did, clamped eyes on the loose version of Harriet. "Hello, again."

"Isn't it *ma*rvelous?" Harriet cried, laying heavy emphasis on the first syllable. Diamond bracelets lined the long, black, satin gloves on her short arms.

Dodo snapped her eyes to David's who shrugged and whispered. "She insisted. Showed up on my doorstep and demanded to come. She'd already had a G and T and a couple of other drinks."

No kidding!

"Are you here alone with her?"

21

"Cripes no! We came with a whole group, but to be honest, Harriet has scared them off with her outrageous drunken behavior. Seeing you was like finding a life buoy in a choppy sea."

Didi appeared at Dodo's elbow. "Hello," she said, all smiles. "David, how lovely." He kissed her glowing cheek.

Smokey Syncopation changed to a fast number that had been popular at the beginning of the year, and the whole room cheered like a crowd at a football stadium as Rupert smoothly slid his arms around Dodo.

"The man of the hour," announced David.

Rupert tapped his nose with a warning look.

"No fear, old chap," said David. "No one will hear it from me."

"Romeo!" shrieked Harriet, startling Dodo. Tonight, she was dressed in a rather drab, gunmetal-gray, drop-waist dress with a matching bandeau, her plain face devoid of makeup. However, the alcohol fueling her mood brightened her eyes so that the animation made her almost pleasant looking. Inhibitions to the wind, she grabbed Rupert around the neck, pulling him down and planting a big smooch right on his lips. He pulled away as if she were a viper.

"Don't be shy!" Harriet squealed, throwing her energies back into the dance. Rupert wiped his mouth roughly with the back of his hand.

Oblivious of the mood she had created, Harriet began gyrating in her own little world.

Dodo frowned.

"Between you and me, she's had three cocktails since we arrived," David explained to Rupert. "I'm no prude, but her behavior is so unpredictable that even *I'm* worried. Don't want her to ruin your evening."

"I can always have a bouncer throw her out," growled Rupert, smarting.

"If it gets to that point, I'll let you know," David agreed and plunged into the crowd in his new role as chaperone.

"Shake it off," said Dodo into Rupert's ear.

Fortunately, Lucille slowed things down with a bone-melting ballad, and Dodo pulled Rupert close. He relaxed into her.

"Sorry," he whispered. "She was just completely out of line."

"I totally agree," replied Dodo as she watched Didi wander over to the food table. "Let's just forget about her."

For the next three minutes they blocked out the rest of the world, and Dodo observed the other revelers as she leaned her cheek against Rupert's chest. The crowd was large, and for the most part she did not recognize anyone, but every so often as Rupert guided her on the dance floor, a familiar face would emerge.

The party had been in full swing for about an hour and Dodo was impressed with the good behavior, but she reasoned it was a result of Rupert's careful planning. The thickset bouncers promptly removed anyone who got out of hand, and in addition, the patrons seemed to appreciate that it was somewhat of an honor to be in attendance—they were careful not to act out. Furthermore, Rupert had successfully created a culture of distinction and high expectations. A winning combination.

The enormous, bald man she had run into on arrival appeared in their periphery as the music returned to fast dance rhythms, and Didi moseyed back. Had Dodo not been paying attention, she would have missed the slight head signal the head bouncer gave to Rupert.

"Excuse me for a moment."

Dodo watched as the two men discussed something. The slightly menacing bouncer was carved out of marble with a tight mustache over his upper lip. He had asked Rupert a question or reported an incident and was now listening intently, the mustache rippling. After a sharp nod he disappeared into the crowd.

"Everything alright?" Dodo asked when Rupert returned to their dancing circle.

"Nothing out of the ordinary. A couple of people getting out of hand were thrown out and put in a taxi."

"How many of these parties have you organized now?" she asked.

"This is my sixth. I learn things from each one and implement changes."

"Such as?"

"I didn't employ heavies for the first one, which was a mistake. The late hour mixed with alcohol and bravado makes for a bad combination at times. Now, I hire ex-soldiers with a sense of decorum to patrol the party. I rarely use the same crew twice. If someone gets out of control, we stuff them into a cab and pay the fare."

"Genius! But this is a rather desolate spot at night. Not too many taxis around."

"I put a flea in the right ears and the drivers line up outside just waiting for fares," Rupert explained.

"You seem to think of everything. Do the bouncers know you are the man behind the event?"

"No. Like I said, I mention a 'boss' all the time to deflect their attention from me but assure them the 'boss' has given me full authority to make decisions. As long as they get paid, they know better than to ask too many questions."

"What about the waiters?"

"Same thing. I ask my contact at the Savoy to suggest a waiter to head up a crew and assemble a group of trustworthy folk who do not work at the hotel. Always a different team. As for the head waiter, I tell them there will be a hefty bonus for discretion and if all runs smoothly. Money is a great motivator. And these are people who are not in a management role at the hotel. They feel it a coup to get the job."

He swung her round, and the tassels on her gown flew out. "If Granny is right and the world as we know it does fall apart, you have a proven means of supporting yourself."

Rupert's blue eyes crinkled at the corners. "I've never thought of it that way, but yes. If I had to, I could replicate this model all over the country. But for the moment, I'm content to keep things local and simple."

As the band transitioned to another fast-paced number, Rupert told her he wanted to check on the bar and food. Dodo drew closer to her sister. Didi's cheeks were flushed from exertion, but she showed no signs of stopping.

"I can't remember the last time I had so much fun dancing," she panted. "Charlie would love it."

"Mmm," Dodo replied as she watched Rupert speak to a stocky, young man wearing a white apron near the food table. The worker ran a hand over his slicked-back, black hair and put a stubby finger to his lips as if considering Rupert's words. Then he nodded tightly and turned on his heel. Rupert returned.

"Everything tickety-boo?" she asked.

"All present and correct." He checked his watch. "The band is due for their first break in five minutes. I just need to make sure the back-up band is ready. I had the waiter put more food and drink in the Green Room for Lucille and company."

"Do what you need to do, darling," said Dodo with a kiss. "I shall keep Didi company."

Smokey Syncopation sounded even better live than on the records she had at home, and she marveled at the resonant quality of Lucille's tone. As the song faded, Dodo noticed another group standing to the side of the stage. A buxom redhead with scarlet lips and a gold dress was giving directions to two other men. As soon as Lulu finished the number, the redhead climbed the few steps and took control of the microphone.

"Good evening, London!" she cried into the mike in an accent that could only be described as Scouse. The crowd roared and clapped as *Smokey Syncopation* took a well-deserved rest and filed off the dais, swallowed by the dark.

"Are we having fun?" the new singer bellowed, throwing a blue boa around her neck. Another roar came from the dancers as the drummer began a background beat. The redhead clapped with the rhythm and soon the whole place was following suit. "We are Crazy Train. My name is Miranda Masters." Everyone cheered. "On the drums, we have Gerry Waters." Gerry waved a drumstick to shouts of delight. Miranda sure knew how to work a crowd.

Seamlessly, the pianist added to the mix and Miranda introduced him. "And on the piano, Fred Garrett." The young, scraggly man stood, still playing, and the crowd applauded. Then to Dodo's shock, Miranda grabbed the stand of the microphone, and in the most velvety, throaty voice, sang the blues. No trace of her Liverpudlian accent. Dodo noticed Lucille look over her shoulder with admiration. This girl may be a nobody, but not for long.

"Fancy a bite or a drink?" she asked Didi as couples closed the gap and swayed in sync to the music.

"Rather!" replied her sister.

They weaved through the bodies and stood in line at the bar. When it was their turn, she ordered pineapple juice for both of them. The angular waiter cocked a brow. "That all, miss?"

"Yes, thank you."

As he filled two glasses, the head waiter she had seen talking to Rupert whispered something in the bartender's ear. The chap looked more like a friendly butcher than a server. She could imagine him in a straw boater standing in a village shop. The bartender nodded to the waiter then handed Dodo the glasses.

Didi knocked hers back. "I was parched!"

"Me too."

They moved away to let others order, and Dodo caught sight of David with Harriet. They were dancing together, but Harriet was draped as though she were asleep standing up, and David's expression of horror made Dodo snicker. He caught her eye and pantomimed his distaste, making Dodo laugh even more.

The slow ballad ended and a much quicker song began. David frog-marched Harriet to one of the few chairs and sat her down, limp as a rag doll. Dodo dragged Didi with her.

"Having fun?" she asked David.

"Dreadful! Simply dreadful, but she's in the sleepy stage now, so I can plant her here and come and dance with you two. That will improve the evening one hundred percent." He laid Harriet across two chairs and then joined the sisters. Grabbing Didi's hand, he spun her round, sending magical laughter spilling from her lips.

They all danced together for another half an hour, and Dodo wondered what had become of Rupert. The redhead did not disappoint with her repertoire, and Dodo was convinced she would soon be a star.

Where was Rupert?

A small commotion near the stage caught Dodo's attention. Lucille was at the bottom of the stairs with Dex and Cy.

"You have been a wonderful audience," purred Miranda into the microphone. "Please give it up for Gerry and Fred. And don't forget our name, Crazy Train."

The oiled crowd cheered and shouted as the two bands swapped places. Dex performed a riff on the saxophone and the crowd went wild. Then Cy matched him with the trumpet, and ear-splitting whistles raised the roof.

Where was Lonnie?

Dodo noticed Lucille cast a nervous eye over her shoulder then begin singing a jazzy tune Dodo had not heard before.

David spun her round and she threw back her head, eyes on the rafters of the old deserted building. Were those dark blobs roosting pigeons?

Her feet were beginning to burn, and she wondered if she could leave Didi with David and find a seat. As she searched the room for a free chair, she spotted Rupert making his way through the crowd, but he was not smiling.

"May I?" he asked David.

"Certainly, old chap." David released her, taking Didi into his arms without hesitation.

Rupert pulled Dodo tight and whispered in her ear. "A waiter just found Lonnie behind the Savoy van. He's been shot."

Chapter 4

Dodo pushed back and in a tense whisper mouthed, "Shot?"

Rupert nodded and grabbed her hand, guiding her across the dance floor, out the side door, past the burly bouncer and into the starry night. Then he led her around the *Savoy* van where a terrified waiter was standing, wide-eyed, face pale in the bright moonlight, standing guard over the body.

"I-I 'aven't m-moved, guv, j-just like you asked me, and n-no one's come out. Will your b-boss come for this?"

"He left the country yesterday," said Rupert. "But I'll take it from here." He reached into his pocket and pulled out some pound notes. "There's no phone nearby. Take one of the taxis out front and go straight to Scotland Yard. Tell them there has been a murder and bring them back. We need them here as soon as possible."

"Will you stop the dance?" the waiter asked, nervously transferring his weight from one foot to the other.

Rupert clutched his neck. "I'm not sure, to be honest. At this point, I don't want to cause a panic, and I don't want anyone to leave since the police will want to question everybody when they arrive. Now, go man, go!"

Like a mouse bolting from a cat convention, he fled, though whether it was haste to perform Rupert's commission or relief at being able to leave the corpse and spooky alley, Dodo could not tell.

"What happened? Was it that waiter who found him?"

Rupert ran a hand down his careworn features. "It was close to time for *Smokey Syncopation* to go back on stage. I slipped into the Green Room to give them the five-minute warning. Only three of them were there. I asked where Lonnie was, and they all explained that he liked to get some fresh air and have a smoke between sets but would be back in time for the next performance. But when they gathered at the stage side, Lonnie was still missing. Lucille told me not to worry; he was often a bit late for the second set and would probably make a grand entrance. She thought maybe he was chatting with someone and would join them on the stage when he heard them start without him. I kept half an eye out for him, but after twenty minutes, when he still hadn't returned, I decided to start a hunt."

That's why Rupert had not returned to the dance floor.

Hand still at his throat, Rupert looked along the alley. "I became frantic, looking behind every door and curtain. I finally ran out to the alley and found that lad, white as a sheet, his mouth working like some oversized goldfish. That's when he pointed to Lonnie. Collapsed behind the van, a bullet to the heart."

"Did you check for a pulse?" she asked.

"Oh, yes! He's dead alright."

Dodo kneeled down to get a better view. The pianist was on his back, head near the van, his signature trilby knocked off and sitting by his head like a guardian. A scarlet stain was spreading across his white shirt as his lifeless eyes stared straight ahead. *Should she close them?*

"Do you have a pencil or pen, or even a comb?"

As Rupert reached into the pocket of his jacket and handed her a pen, she noticed a white feather stuck to the bottom of his shoe. Using the pen, she pushed back the piano player's coat. She wiggled the pen around in the inside breast pocket and felt a card. Withdrawing it carefully, she found a sepia photograph of a beautiful, young, black woman. She turned it over. Nothing. Replacing the picture, she began to draw an imaginary line around the body as she had once seen an inspector do. Lonnie's hands were clenched. She pried them open, but they were empty. His hands remained open as she withdrew the pen. No rigor, which was to be expected. The bottoms of his shoes were wet, which wasn't surprising since she and Didi had got their own feet wet when they arrived, but looking around the van, she saw no puddles. So, perhaps he had ventured farther than this part of the alley. By his trouser leg, she found a lit cigarette with a long arm of ash and a spent match. She remembered that Lucille and the others had said that was why Lonnie went outside, for fresh air and a smoke.

The killer must have surprised him.

Continuing her outline of the body, she stopped at his left trouser cuff. Remnants of a white powder were evident. She bent low to smell it. No odor.

Moving up his side with the pen, she spotted a stain on his white collar, and leaning in concluded that it was reddish lipstick. She also caught the faint scent of rose water.

Before she stood, Dodo pushed the pen against his cheek. It was soft and malleable.

"It cannot have happened too long ago," she said, the sounds of the band muted by the thick walls. "Rigor mortis has not begun, and the blood is still flowing and crimson. Besides, you saw him alive less than twenty minutes ago. Did you look for signs of anyone else out here?" She looked around as if the murderer might be lingering, watching their investigation.

"I ran around the other side of the building and out to the front before coming to get you. I didn't see anyone and it's frankly too dark to see footprints."

Dodo walked a slow circle. Looking along the edges of the walls, she came upon a small pile of cigarette butts. It could be a clue, but they could also have been there for ages. She used the pen to push them apart. They were dry.

"Rupert! Hand me a handkerchief." She picked up one of the used cigarettes from the pile. Smelling it, she winced. French. The strong, unique tobacco of the Gauloises cigarette was still fragrant. She would point it out to the inspector when he arrived. The pile indicated the killer had been waiting for some time before Lonnie exited.

"What should I do now?" asked Rupert. "Nothing like this has ever happened before. I'm concerned we could have a frightened mob on our hands."

"Perhaps you could tell the bouncers to ask people to stay if they make to leave but not tell them why at this point. Then wait for the police to arrive. And you can't exactly tell the band in the middle of their performance."

Dodo thought about her reasoning that someone wasn't truly dead until those who cared about them knew about it.

"Let's hope they get here quickly," she muttered, thinking that it was about six miles to Scotland Yard, and at this time of night the streets would be empty. There and back twelve miles. At least twenty minutes. Maybe ten had passed since the waiter left.

"You go and I'll stay here with the body," she said.

"Not bally likely!" Rupert spluttered. "The murderer could still be out here, Dodo. No. Why don't you go and get David to stay out here with you while I—well, I don't really know what I'm going to do. I'll ad lib."

"Are you sure?"

"I'm sure."

She gave Rupert a quick kiss and hurried back inside the warehouse, past the heavy bouncer. The knowledge of the murder was like a hot potato hidden in her chest, a secret that only she knew—a secret that would change everything. A visitor to their country had been struck down.

Murdered.

The jolly sound of the band and the gyrating bodies were all at odds with the sad circumstances outside as she weaved her way around the floor until she found David, who was still dancing with Didi.

"Dodo, where have you been?" asked Didi as she twirled and bobbed.

"I need to steal your partner," she said in as chipper a voice as she could manage.

"Me?" asked David, stopping mid-twirl.

"Yes, you. There's something I simply must show you."

David's features formed into a Cheshire-cat grin. "Curious," he purred.

She grabbed his hand, waving goodbye to her sister, and dragged David toward the door on the side of the building where the body lay.

"Hold on!" protested David. "Why are you in such a hurry?"

When they got to the door, she stood on tiptoe to whisper in his ear. "I need your help. It is rather gory. Can you handle it?"

He clasped her by the wrists. "Do you mean...?"

All business, she nodded.

The happy-go-lucky expression slid from his face like butter off a hot scone. Fear stepped into its place. "It's one thing to hear about murders, but it is quite another to see one."

"Shall I find someone else?"

He dragged a hand across his mouth. "No! I can do this."

"I don't need anyone going wobbly on me," she warned.

He swallowed hard. "You can count on me." His eyes flared. "Is there m-much blood?"

"I'm afraid there is," she responded.

David ran both hands down his luxurious jacket and declared, "I'm ready."

Opening the door, they left the hustle and bustle of the dance behind until it was no more than an eerie echo.

"This way," she encouraged.

As they rounded the van, Rupert looked up with haunted eyes. "Thank goodness! I was getting rattled out here alone with only the rats for company."

David was staring at the prostrate, bloodied body of the musician. Dodo witnessed the telltale rise and fall of his stomach. "Are you going to be sick, David?"

Sucking in large gulps of air, David put a hand to his head. "I think I'll be alright."

"Look, I have to go back inside to talk to the bouncers," said Rupert. "But we can't leave the body alone, and I didn't want Dodo out here by herself. Are you up to the task, David?"

David dragged his eyes from the body and stared into Rupert's face with alarmed eyes. "You can count on me."

"Good! The police should be here any second. Then we'll have a real problem on our hands." He disappeared around the van leaving Dodo and David alone.

The lapping of the river against the banks and the occasional hoot of an owl stoked the eerie atmosphere.

David's wild eyes connected with the corpse again. "It's the piano player," he murmured.

"Yes, it is."

"What do you think happened?" he asked Dodo.

"It's very early on, but it looks like Lonnie came out for a smoke and was shot at point-blank range. He either knew his attacker or he was surprised from behind and turned around before being shot. I also believe the killer was waiting for some time, since there is a pile of dry butts over by that wall." She pointed.

David's teeth started to chatter. "You c-can t-tell all th-that?"

"Well, there is a warm cigarette right next to the body, he's on his back and his eyes were open in shock."

"Dodo, you are an enigma. N-no one would suspect your penchant for detection just by l-looking at you."

"I'm not sure if I should be flattered or offended," she responded.

34

Dodo tipped her head. The quiet sounds of the early morning had been joined by the faint sound of a police bell ringing.

Chapter 5

"Thank heavens for that!" cried David as the ringing came closer. "I don't mind telling you I am more than a little daunted about being alone out here with this...poor fellow. I don't know how you do it, Dodo."

Fingering the pearl in her lobe, she admitted, "Honestly, neither do I." Then she held David by the arms. "I'm just going to flag the police down so they know where we are. Alright?"

David blanched but nodded, and Dodo ran out into the street.

When the first of the black vehicles pulled to a screeching stop, an older man in his late fifties climbed out, placing a brown hat over his salt-and-pepper, slicked-back hair.

"Harris! Question those cabbies out front. See if they saw anything."

"Sir!"

Dodo held out her hand. "Lady Dorothea Dorchester. Let me take you to the body."

Before shaking hands, he looked her up and down with cynical eyes. His grip was firm, and his hand engulfed hers. "Inspector Crenshaw. Lead on."

David was jumping from one foot to the other, his eyes hectic.

"And you are?" asked the irritable policeman.

"David. Bellamy. David Bellamy."

Dodo had never seen David so undone and had to squash a smile.

The inspector dropped down beside the corpse with a slight grunt. David jerked his head towards the building, eyes wide, lips clamped.

"Do you need David out here, Inspector Crenshaw? He was just keeping me company," explained Dodo.

From his crouching position, the inspector looked up and squinted. "I shall want a statement."

"Of course. I'll wait inside. Tata." David sprinted for the side door that was now guarded by a constable and didn't look back.

"Do you know him?" the inspector asked, still examining the body over his pot belly.

"*Know* is a bit of an exaggeration. His name is Lonnie Chapman. He's a member of the jazz band playing here tonight, and I only met him right before the party started."

"Jazz band?"

"Smokey Syncopation. They're quite popular, Inspector."

His unremarkable face screwed into a state of incomprehension, causing his mustache to push into his nose.

"They're American," she explained. "From New Orleans in Louisiana."

"Ahh," he said, nodding, his bottom lip jutting out and tugging at the bristly mustache. "American. Who found him?"

"One of the waiters," Dodo replied.

"I shall need to speak to him first."

"Would you like me to try to find him?"

Suddenly, the music from inside the building stopped short. The muffled, gruff tone of another policeman could be heard, though the individual words were difficult to decipher.

"The waiter should be easy enough to find, but thanks for the offer." He nodded toward the warehouse. "I told them to stop the entertainment and tell everyone to stay in the building." Pushing his hat back, he sighed. "There'll be no sleep for us tonight."

Inspector Crenshaw was very thorough, but the light from the moon was not strong enough. "Pritchett!" he cried.

A younger policeman in uniform came running from the street. "Sir?"

"I need your torch."

The constable handed over the torch that was hanging from his belt, and the inspector swung the beam across Lonnie's lifeless face. The features that had been so jolly and friendly mere hours before were now fixed and blank.

The inspector stopped at Lonnie's trouser cuff, pointing the beam at the white powder. He paused, then bent to sniff it as she had done. Continuing up, he paused at the pianist's open hands. Dodo thought about confessing that she had pried them open but considering the inspector's dour mood, decided against it. Besides, she had done it to see if there was anything clutched between his fingers, and there wasn't.

The beam continued its journey, following Lonnie's contours, and paused at the cigarette, then stopped near his collar. The stain Dodo had observed showed bright pink in the light of the torch.

"Well, well, well," murmured the inspector. "Did Mr. Chapman have a girlfriend?"

"Not that I'm aware of, but as I said, I only met him for the first time tonight. However, the singer of the band is a woman. A very beautiful woman."

"Name?"

"Lucille Bassett." Dodo took a chance. "Can you smell the rose water, Inspector?"

He leaned in. "Yes."

"Lucille was wearing a much stronger scent this evening. It is not a brand I recognize and is quite possibly only available in America."

He quirked an eyebrow at Dodo. "Anything else you noticed?"

38

"I'm sure you spotted the dead match and half-smoked cigarette by his side. That indicates that he was smoking when he was shot."

The inspector frowned. "This *is* a dock. That cigarette could have been here for months."

"Oh, I don't think so, Inspector. If you look, the ash is intact and the cigarette itself is quite dry. It was raining earlier today and would be sodden if it had been here long before tonight."

"Humpph," said the inspector, straightening up, his knees cracking.

"And over there," she pointed to the side of the building. "I found a small pile of French cigarettes that were also quite dry. I would wager his assailant was waiting for him to come out, which implies that the killer was someone who knew the building and Lonnie's habits and that he was waiting a rather long time."

The inspector's eyes descended into a deep frown. "Who are you again?"

"Lady Dorothea Dorchester. You might remember me from the case of the murdered model at the British Empire Fair or the member of parliament who was accused of impersonation and murder."

Swiping off his hat, the inspector brushed an arm across his brow. "Well, I'm blowed! I do remember the one about the MP. My boss worked that case before his promotion. I heard he worked with some toff—I do beg your pardon, m'lady. I heard he worked with a lady. So that was you, eh?"

Dodo sucked in her cheeks. "Yes, that was me."

A noise interrupted them, and a constable approached with Rupert, who took off his jacket and placed it around Dodo's shoulders.

"Allow me to introduce Mr. Rupert Danforth, Inspector Crenshaw. The organizer of the jazz party."

The two men shook hands.

"So, this is *your* party?" asked the inspector.

"Yes," replied Rupert, "Though no one inside knows that."

"Care to explain?"

Rupert gave an abbreviated history to the inspector, who blew out a whistle. "I've got to hand it to you. That's quite an accomplishment."

"Thank you. And until tonight we have taken care of any problems in-house. When I say problems, I mean arguments over girls or people drinking too much. We've never had anything quite like a murder before."

Several more police vehicles pulled into the street, and various policeman spilled out.

"Everyone's inside," shouted Inspector Crenshaw. "We've told them all to stay put. Higgins is organizing everybody so they can be questioned. Go inside and take your orders from him. Standard interview. Off you go."

The officers all crunched around to the large doors at the front of the building.

"Right. I think I've seen all I need to out here." Crenshaw blew air between his teeth, producing an ear-splitting whistle.

Dodo flinched.

Yet another policeman in uniform, this one looking ready to retire any day, came ambling up the alley.

"Sir!" His voice held the tune of a thousand cigarettes.

"Stay with the body until the detail with the stretcher arrives. They shouldn't be long now."

"Yessir!"

Turning to Rupert, he asked, "Is there somewhere we can talk?"

Rupert headed back into the warehouse, and they slipped into the dark, cavernous space. Hundreds of voices raised in complaint now replaced the sweet sounds of jazz as Rupert, Dodo and the inspector ducked along the edge and behind the black curtain to the Green Room. Lucille was sitting bent over, Dex patting her back, his face long as a bass player's bow. Lucille looked up, eyes red with tears, makeup tracking down her flawless cheeks.

"Is it true?" she asked in her patented, smoky, southern accent.

"I'm afraid so," said Dodo coming to take her hand. "But he would have died instantly if that's any comfort."

"We haven't even been in England long enough to make any enemies. I can't help thinking it was all a big mistake. That they thought he was someone else." She wiped her eyes with a lacy handkerchief smelling of roses.

"That may yet turn out to be the case," said Dodo, though she thought it highly unlikely.

Inspector Crenshaw approached. "I assume you are Miss Lucille Bassett."

"I am," she said, a cracked, heartbroken smile materializing through her tears. "And to whom do I have the pleasure of speaking?"

"My name is Inspector Crenshaw, ma'am. I'm so sorry that your friend has been killed. I'm going to interview Mr. Danforth, here, and then I should like to talk to you."

"Anything you say, Inspector. Lonnie was one of my dearest friends."

The inspector and Rupert secured a corner of the room, and Rupert dragged a couple of chairs over. They sat in intense, quiet conversation.

Dodo was still holding Lucille's gloved hand with its triple band of pearls. "How long have you known Lonnie?"

The famous singer's lip quivered. "He was a close friend of my daddy's. They were like brothers. I can't remember a time when he wasn't around somewhere. He became a sort of guardian when Daddy died."

"And your mother?"

Long, black lashes swept the curvy, velvet cheek. "My mama died when I was eleven years old, giving birth to my little brother."

"Oh, I'm so sorry," said Dodo.

"It's all right. It was a long time ago. Daddy took good care of us. His father was a cotton picker. Long hours in the beatin' sun. Daddy didn't want to do that his whole life. When he was thirteen, he found an old trumpet in the trash. It was all beat up, but he took it home and started teachin' himself to play. Saw it as a way off the plantation." She dabbed at her eyes. "In the 80s, Daddy played for a brass band. That's where he met Lonnie. Then a guy, name of Buddy Bolden, started a new type of band in 1895 and invited Daddy and Lonnie to join him. It was the early sounds of jazz." She closed her eyes as if she had just eaten a piece of rich chocolate. "It was a sound like nothing else. I used to sneak into their practices and sing along—no words you understand. Just scat."

"Scat?" It was a word Dodo had never heard.

"Music from the soul." Fist to her chest, aching sounds, so rich in timbre, sliding up and down the scale, escaped Lucille's mouth. "Like that." She went quiet and wiped her cheek. "Daddy heard me one day, washing the clothes out back. He marched me to the church choir and insisted they take me on. I was twelve at the time. Within months I was the soloist. I learned all I know 'bout singin' from Miss Bonnie Rose, God rest her soul."

Lucille cast miserable eyes over to the corner of the room where Inspector Crenshaw was still interviewing Rupert. "Lonnie and Daddy had started a band on their own, and when I was old enough, Daddy asked me to be the singer. We played on Bourbon Street every weekend and Tuesday nights.

"Then, when I was twenty-five, Daddy had a heart attack. I thought my life was over until Lonnie took me and my brother under his wing. The rest is history." Her face collapsed. "And now Lonnie is gone. I just can't believe it!"

Dodo put an arm around her shoulders.

Dex pattered over, his cheeks shiny. "Sakes! Lonnie! Makes me want to play the blues."

"Me too, Dex. Me too," murmured Lucille.

"How did *you* join the band?" Dodo asked him.

"I was just a ratty, old street kid when Lonnie heard me busking. He took pity on me and became my mentor. I was playing an old, beat-up saxophone for pennies on the street corner hoping to make enough to eat each day. I think Lonnie saw a bit of himself in me and took me in. Paid for lessons too."

Lonnie was beginning to sound like a saint. Dodo turned in her seat.

"What about you, Cy?"

Cy touched his scar. "After Mr. Bassett died, the band needed another trumpet player. They held auditions and three hundred people tried out. They were already somethin' big in N'Orleans. I never thought I stood a chance, but Lucille here, she heard something in my tone that reminded her of her Daddy, and I got the job." He bunched up his lips and his eyes winked in the dim light.

Dodo checked that the inspector was still busy with Rupert. "So, what happened during the break? Did you all stay together?"

"We came in here and ate some of the food," began Cy. "I don't know where Mr. Rupert got it, but it was mighty fine stuff. Anyways, we were just sitting around reminiscing and making fun of London—no offense intended, but it couldn't be more different from Louisiana, and we are freezin' cold most of the time."

"None taken," Dodo responded.

"Anyways, Lonnie, he likes being outside when he can and told us he was going out for a smoke. Happens all the time. Calms his fingers. We just let him go." His voice caught on the last word, and he choked back some tears.

Dex took over. "When he wasn't here by the time we were due back on, we didn't think much of it and figured

43

he'd join in when he was done with his cigarette. It's happened before."

The door to the Green Room slammed open and Dodo gasped, but it was the back-up band, Crazy Train.

"We're being treated like common criminals out there," complained Miranda. "They're saying someone's been shot."

The inspector cried out from the corner, "Keep it down over there."

Dodo beckoned to Miranda and her musicians. "It's true. Lonnie Chapman."

Miranda's face blanched. "They wouldn't tell us who." She ran toward Lucille. "I'm so sorry."

The contrast between the two women was stark, but each was stunning in her own way. Dodo moved to let Miranda get closer.

"What happened?" Miranda asked.

Lucille shook her head. "We don't even know. We were simply told he's gone."

"The rumors are true. He was shot," clarified Dodo as gently as she could.

"Shot? What on earth...?" sobbed Lucille.

"From what I saw, it looked like someone was waiting for him. Like it was someone who knew him and his habits," Dodo revealed.

Lucille's ebony eyes snapped up full of fire. "Just what are you suggestin' little lady?"

"I'm suggesting nothing. I'm merely telling you there is evidence that indicates someone was waiting."

"Evidence?" Lucille was becoming hysterical, and Inspector Crenshaw cast a worried eye in her direction. Time to dial things back.

"When did you arrive in England?" Dodo asked.

"Three days ago." Lucille was finding it difficult to control her temper. "We thought that would be enough time

44

to get acclimated before our first performance. We slid this show in before our tour."

It had not occurred to Dodo that the band would have a full schedule of performances because her mind had been otherwise engaged, but now it was obvious that they would not travel this far for one concert.

"Did you use an agent? What is his name?"

Lucille took a shaky breath. "A Mr. Neville Spoonbridge out of Birming*ham*."

She laid emphasis on the last syllable, and Dodo wanted to cringe but curbed the urge.

"He wrote to us last year," Lucille continued, "and suggested we broaden our exposure—I believe that's the phrase he used, because it made Lonnie and I laugh—by coming to Great Britain. We'd been thinking of going international anyway and his letter came at a good time. Lonnie and I made all such decisions together, and we started up a correspondence with Mr. Spoonbridge. Lonnie taught me everything he knew about the business side of things so that when he was gone…" her words evaporated into sobs.

"Miss Bassett," called the inspector as Rupert got up from the chair.

Lucille traded looks with Miranda, stiffened her spine and stalked over to the inspector, head high.

Chapter 6

Frazzled and weary, Rupert finally left the inspector and made way for Lucille. Dodo looked at her watch. It was now past three in the morning. The rush of excitement had long since departed, killing the romanticism of the atmosphere and reducing the Green Room to a stark, dusty afterthought. Dodo felt the drag of fatigue pulling her down like a millstone.

She reached out her hands for him. Taking them, he said, "I'm glad that's over. Now, I need to go back out there." He glanced at the doorway that separated them from the throngs in the main space. "I must settle up and send the staff home."

"Didi!" cried Dodo. "I totally forgot she's out there. Do you think the inspector would mind if I left to find her?"

"It's not like you're going home. I'll vouch for you. Come on! Let's face this thing together."

Careful not to draw attention, they slid through the door and into the dance area. Instead of the steady beat of hypnotic jazz, the only melody was the continued hum of irritation and confusion. The mood lights did little to brighten the tiresome proceedings.

Stations had been set up in the four corners, with a police officer in each area and groups of people for them to question. The numbers had dwindled a little, indicating that after questioning, people were free to leave.

Rupert and Dodo parted company as he set off to find his temporary employees, and she to search for Didi. Eventually, she found her with David on the far side of the room.

"Dodo!" said Didi with relief. She lowered her voice. "David told me what happened. Awful!"

David had still not regained his usual glowing countenance.

"Have you been interviewed yet?" Dodo asked them.

"I haven't, but David has," Didi explained, twisting a delicate pearl bracelet around her wrist.

It was odd for Dodo to see this taciturn version of her usually high-spirited friend.

"Bally terrible, is all I have to say," gushed David. "My esteem for your straight-headedness has increased in leaps and bounds, and in future I will stick to the gossipy side of things. Turns out I don't actually like getting my hands dirty."

"Poor David!" said Dodo with an exaggerated pout.

"You're next," said a girl in a loose, tasseled dress to Didi.

"Wish me luck!" Her sister raised a hand as she walked over to be questioned.

Dodo directed her next comment to David. "What did the officer ask you?"

"At first his questions were extremely general. Why was I here? Who was I with? So, I thought I'd get the ball rolling by admitting that I had stood guard over the body."

"Are they not telling people there has been a murder?" she asked quietly.

"Not as far as I can tell. Probably don't want to create a panic. They're just asking if you went outside at all, what time, and if you saw anything odd. Then they take your name and address and telephone number if you have one."

"What did the copper say when you told him about minding the body?"

"He almost dropped his pencil and asked me to keep the matter confidential. Which I did. Except for Didi."

Dodo looked around. "Where is dear Lady Harriet?"

David's mouth shrugged, and he pointed to a couple of chairs where lay the reposed figure of his companion for the evening. "I quite envy her at this point," he breathed. "I

47

shall never get that terrible image out of my head." He jabbed Dodo in the shoulder. "If I get nightmares, I'm blaming you."

"I thought you might be honored to help," she responded.

"Well, I was at first. But at such a cost. Never again!" There was no hint of his usual jocularity.

"How are you going to get Harriet home?" Dodo asked.

"Perhaps Rupert can help me carry her into a taxi. She's a dead weight. Plus, she's in no condition to be interviewed. I've already given her details to the policeman."

"I think Rupert will be tied up for some time. Between the three of us we should be able to manage it. Let's wait for Didi to be done."

Bewilderment decorated the faces of the partygoers as they finished up their interviews and left in small groups. They would find out what it was all about soon enough from the morning papers if the rumors hadn't already got around the room.

"Too bad the bar has shut up shop. I could do with a stiff drink right about now," declared David.

Didi rejoined them.

"That was quick!" remarked Dodo.

"They're not saying much," replied Didi, "and I pretended not to know anything. And besides, I did not leave the building at all during the evening and pointed out several people who could verify my statement. Then he asked for my name and address, and it was over."

"Good! Now, we have to help David get Harriet into a taxi."

Didi frowned.

The crowd had thinned considerably, and though it seemed almost cruel to wake her, their departure was overdue.

David shook Harriet's shoulder.

Nothing. She could be another corpse but for her chapped cheeks and unladylike snoring.

Placing his hands under her back, David pulled Harriet to a sitting position, and Dodo noticed her mouth was smudged with red lipstick. Her head lolled to the side, and she murmured something slightly scandalous but did not awaken. He placed one of her limp arms around his own shoulders and Dodo did the same on the other side while Didi held her upright from the rear.

Harriet's legs were useless, so they dragged her through the door and outside where a crowd of people were waiting for more taxis to arrive. Her flagrant intoxication drew some judgmental stares. Dodo checked the time. It was now four o'clock. Their own car should be there by now.

"Didi, go and look for the Bentley. I think I can hold Harriet up for the moment."

Didi headed out to the street while Dodo and David bent under the weight of Harriet.

Hurry up!

Within seconds Didi was back, waving at them to follow her. They dragged Harriet past the waiting couples and Dodo was flooded with relief to see the family car. The chauffeur was already out with the back door wide open.

"Brown, would you mind taking Mr. Bellamy and his guest, Lady Harriet Plumford, home? Lady Diantha and I need to stay here a little longer. I hope we will be ready to leave by the time you return."

"Of course, m'lady." If he was surprised at the state of Lady Harriet, he did not show it. British servants were brilliant at discretion.

Dodo lifted Harriet's arm from her own shoulder, releasing a cloud of rose water scent from the girl, and David took the full weight as he laid her carefully across the seat. The chauffeur walked around the car and gently pulled Lady Harriet further in from the other side.

49

David wiped his brow with a handkerchief and hugged Dodo. "What a night! Your man certainly knows how to put on a show!"

"What a night, indeed!" she responded. "Now, go home and get some well-deserved sleep."

David jumped into the passenger seat and waved as they pulled away.

"You can really tell what people are made of in a crisis," Dodo said as they watched the sleek car disappear into the inky darkness.

"I know," agreed Didi. "He was an absolute wreck when he found me after seeing the body."

Several taxis were now lined up and jaded patrons jumped in, eager to get away from an evening that had started with such promise. Dodo hoped the murder would not tarnish Rupert's thriving business. However, if she had learned anything about human nature in the last couple of years, it was that tragedy was more likely to increase the popularity of something.

Dodo and her sister wandered back into the warehouse that was now less than half-filled. Rupert came toward them, lines of anxiety etched on his handsome face.

"What a bally mess!" he declared. "The staff have all been interviewed and are packing up the leftovers."

"What about the band members?" she asked.

"Honestly, I've been too busy to check. Would you mind?"

"Of course not. Come on, Didi. Let's take care of the talent."

Rupert strode off to put out another fire, and she and Didi slipped behind the curtain and into the Green Room. The inspector was in the process of interviewing the drummer of *Crazy Train*, Gerry Waters, and Miranda and Lucille were sitting in stunned silence in two of the chairs.

Dodo did a double take. Miranda was wearing a wig. It had shifted a little in all the commotion to reveal thin, mouse-colored hair beneath.

On seeing Dodo, Lucille looked up with expectation. "We've all been interviewed. Can we go?"

"I don't see why not. You can settle up with Rupert later."

Lucille drew a delicate, lace stole around her shoulders. "Oh, he paid us in advance, honey."

"Do you have your own car?" Dodo asked. She hadn't seen one parked.

"No! I wouldn't trust myself or any of us to drive on the wrong side of the road." A half-hearted smile tugged at her lips. "We hired a limo. Told the driver to come back at dawn. What time is it now?"

Dodo checked her watch. "Just before half past four. Dawn will arrive in less than half an hour, I would guess."

"Good. I'm plum tuckered!" declared Lucille. "I just want to get to my own room and mourn in private. I've seen way too much death for one lifetime." A storm cloud had settled across Lucille's soft features, rendering them lined and harsh. "Cy, honey. Can you see if our limo has arrived?"

"Sho'thing, Miss Bassett." The sax player shuffled across the room and disappeared.

A small smile kissed Lucille's sad lips. "Even after all this time, he still calls me Miss Bassett." She huffed and shook her head.

"Where are you staying?" asked Miranda. "We're at Partridges." It was a mid-level hotel in the east end of London, not too far from the docks.

"The Carlton." Lucille raised her brows. "Wouldn't be allowed in such a fancy establishment back home. It's one of the things I like about London."

"One day *I* will be famous enough to stay there," mused Miranda.

51

Lucille cocked her head and pushed out her bottom lip. "From what I just heard, it won't be long, darlin'. You have some pipes!"

A touch of color blossomed over Miranda's round features. "Do you really think so?"

"I know so. You have a tone no voice lessons can create. Pure God-given talent, and that's a fact. You keep singing and someone will soon take notice. You're destined for great things, young lady."

"That means so much to me," said Miranda with no small amount of humility.

"Is that your real name?" asked Lucille, as she made to leave.

A cynical smirk appeared on Miranda's face as she rearranged the auburn wig. "I wish! My given name is Edna Smith. I knew that wasn't taking me nowhere. So, I reinvented myself as Miranda Masters."

"It's a good choice. You're smart and you're talented. With that voice and the right songs, you'll go far."

Cy reappeared. "Limo's here, Miss Bassett."

"Time for me to go." She turned to Dodo. "The inspector has asked us to stay in London for the time being. Let's all get together in a few days, huh?"

"I would like that very much," said Miranda.

"Me too," agreed Dodo.

Chapter 7

Miranda perked up. "That Lucille, she's a class act. Means the world to me that we covered for them." She clasped her hands under her chin. "The stuff of my dreams. Too bad—well, you know." She smiled sheepishly, seeming to realize that her comments might be considered ill-timed.

"How did you get your start?" Dodo asked, seeing the occasion as an opportunity to conduct her own interview.

"Down the local pub, if you must know. Soon as I was twenty-one, Dad paid the owner to let me sing. After a bit the landlord stopped asking for payment. Business was up 'cause people came to hear me sing. It was just my dad on the piano and me, for a bit. Then we were found by Gerry. He was with a band that played at weddings and stuff, but he was bored stiff. He added his smooth drums to the mix, and we sounded a lot more professional.

"One night, a scout was at the pub and came to talk to Gerry and me after our set. Wanted to be our agent but said we'd have to ditch my dad. I said no chance, but when I told Dad about it, he asked me who the agent was. I told him, and what the bloke had said and how I thought he was out of order. But my dad agreed. With the agent! He said he was getting too old for it all and worried that he was holding us back. He said we should put an ad in the paper for another, younger pianist.

"So, we did. Fred came in looking like a tramp. His brother had heard about the auditions and told him to try out. We almost turned him away, but when he touched those keys, it was like magic. Dad let him rent a room for a few months and we tidied him up a bit. Before long, we started turning people down for local gigs 'cause there weren't enough days in a week. That's when Fred moved out. He finally had enough money to live on his own.

"Since then, we've tried our luck further and further south and things are just getting better and better."

"How did you secure this appearance?" Dodo asked.

"Cousin o' mine is a waiter at the Savoy. He's the head waiter here tonight. Sam. After he was asked if he wanted the job, and he accepted, he found out they was looking for a cover band to give the headliner a break. He thought I should put my name in the hat. What did we have to lose? You could have knocked me down with a feather when we got picked. And I never dreamed it was for someone as famous as Smokey Syncopation! They had kept that secret tight as a drum!"

The recollection of the rush of excitement when they had been chosen animated her features.

"It was all very hush hush. We had to sign some legal papers that said we wouldn't tell anyone who we signed with and who the other band was." Her mouth shrugged. "Happy to do it. This thing is the hottest social event on the London calendar from what I hear. And it's great exposure with the toffs. They's the ones with the money, ain't they? We're going to drop a new record in about a week, and I bet our sales skyrocket 'cause of all this. It's bound to be in the papers, right? Could be our golden goose." Her face sagged a little. "Too bad such a terrible thing happened. But life goes on, don't it?"

Dodo tried to drum up sympathy for the girl who was a rising star and on track to surge above her poor upbringing, but the vision of Lonnie in a pool of his own blood dampened her empathy. She was saved from having to speak platitudes when Rupert came back into the room looking utterly exhausted.

"Are you almost done with the inspector?" he asked.

"He's just finishing up with Gerry. Lucille and her crew left about a quarter of an hour ago. How's it looking out there?" Dodo asked.

"Pretty much done." He sighed and struggled against a yawn as Gerry ambled over.

"Can we go now?" Miranda asked the inspector who waved a hand in the affirmative.

"Tell your boss thanks for us," said Miranda, addressing Rupert and slipping on a white cape. "Fancy him missing out on all the drama. Anyway, I'm really grateful. Tata!"

With a quick glance at Dodo, Rupert responded. "You can count on it, Miss Masters. I'll fill him in on every detail. I'm only sorry the evening was cut short for you. I'll be sure to recommend your band for the next date as compensation."

"'Cor, yeah! I mean, I'll talk it over with the lads and see if we can fit it into our busy calendar." She held up a hand dripping with bangles and rings. Rupert kissed it.

"Good night."

"I think it's good morning now, luv," Miranda said with a laugh. Then she turned on her heel and minced her way out of the room, Fred and Gerry trailing behind her like obedient puppies.

The inspector pushed himself out of the chair and wandered over, poking his ear with a finger.

"Anything of interest?" Dodo asked.

"Several things that bear looking into further," he said, ambiguously. "And then there are the things that seem insignificant now that can prove to be critical to the case."

"Such as?" asked Dodo.

"That white powder for a start. Could be chalk from a pool hall. Could be cocaine. You never know." He ran a hand over his round stomach. "And whose lipstick was that on his collar? It looked like a match to both Miranda and Lucille's lipstick. But then again, half the women here were probably wearing the same color. I've got a lot of work ahead of me."

"Does anyone smoke French cigarettes?" she persisted.

The jaded inspector took a deep breath. "They're almost all smokers of one kind or another but no one admitted to smoking that French stuff. English lads tend to stick to more local brands, and I couldn't smell it on any of them. And how would Americans get hold of them? But who knows if they were telling the truth?" He put his hat back on his head and pocketed his notebook. "Right. I think that's all for now. If you don't mind, I'm going to see if I can get in a few hours of shut eye before I have to be back in the office."

"That's a good point," said Dodo as they watched the inspector gather up his officers and depart. "The Green Room did not smell of the Gauloises cigarettes at all."

Chapter 8

A noise woke Dodo.

Disoriented, she raised her head. She must have fallen asleep on the sofa in her mother's cozy sitting room.

"Oh, my darling! I'm so sorry! I didn't know you were in here," exclaimed Lady Dorchester, turning to leave.

"No, it's alright. I needed to wake up anyway. What time is it?"

"Half past three," replied her mother, curling up in her favorite chair.

Dodo rubbed the sleep from her eyes. She and Didi had finally arrived home at seven o'clock that morning. If she had taken any extra clothes to London, she would have stayed in her mother's lavish London flat in Knightsbridge.

Instead, they had come home to Beresford House, and Dodo had slept fitfully until ten. Though she had tried to go back to sleep, her concern for Rupert and his business kept running through her mind and she had finally given up. In an effort to divert her attention, she had been looking through some sketches Renée had brought over from Paris. But she must have dozed off. She leaned over to pick up the drawings from where they had fallen on the floor.

"Did you have a fun evening?" asked her mother, pulling a box of chocolates toward her.

Dodo needed to craft her answer carefully. Lady Guinevere did not *do* murder. She knew that Dodo was involved in criminal investigations of one sort or another, but she refused to hear anything about them. Lady Guinevere would not even read the newsy parts of the paper, fishing out the society pages only. She was quite happy pretending that such things as murder did not happen.

"It was extremely interesting," began Dodo. "Rupert is so clever. His bashes are a highlight of the social calendar. Have you heard of Smokey Syncopation?"

"You'd have to be living under a rock not to," said Lady Guinevere with her sunny laugh. "There are pictures of them all over the society pages. They're staying in London right now, I understand. I think Daddy is trying to get tickets for us to see them at the Palladium." She offered the open box to Dodo, but her mouth was cottony, and she shook her head.

Dare I tell Mummy it will be canceled?

"Rupert booked them for his party!" she declared.

"Did he, now? The dear boy must have a splendid reputation. How very shrewd of him." She popped in a chocolate, her face showing contentment as the treat melted in her mouth.

"I know. I believe I have grossly underestimated him!" replied Dodo.

"What is Miss Bassett like? Did you meet her?" asked her mother with eager eyes.

"Oh, Mummy! She is a character but so approachable. Did you know her grandfather grew up in the cotton fields?"

Lady Guinevere was scanning the box for a second treat and looked up. "No! How did they get into performing music?"

Dodo related the story of the old, beaten-up trumpet.

"Cream always rises to the top," Lady Guinevere commented.

It was one of her mother's many mottos.

"Lucille sounds even better in person than on the gramophone," Dodo continued. "And she is terribly plucky. She poked fun at my nickname and then apologized and asked me to call her Lulu."

Her mother's face registered shock. "I would call that rude."

58

"It didn't feel rude," Dodo responded. "She was just being transparently honest. I liked her a lot. And there was another, less well-known English band that played while Smokey Syncopation took a break. Crazy Train. They're from Liverpool. Oh, Mummy, you are sure to know who they are soon, as the singer has the most fabulous voice. Even Lucille, Miss Bassett, was impressed."

Closing the chocolate box, her mother asked, "And what time did you get in?"

"Very late. Rupert has to direct the staff in the cleanup and settle any bills. Then he must count the money and drop it into the night deposit at the bank."

"I don't know how he does it all," said Lady Guinevere. "I would just pay someone else to manage the whole thing."

"I suppose it's because he wants to keep it a secret that he's the brains behind the parties. If he manages the events, he has more control. Even the bands don't know he is really in charge."

"Ooh, what do you have there?" asked her mother noticing the sketches.

"Next season's proposed collection. Here, take a look."

Rupert spooned the last of his crème brûlée into Dodo's mouth. *Heaven.*

They were at a small restaurant in Little Puddleton pouring over an article on the murder in the newspaper.

"It just says 'in the area of the Docklands'," said Rupert. "And that Lonnie was performing at a private party. Nothing about me, thankfully, and nothing about the powder on his trouser leg or the lipstick. It does say he was shot."

"Have they found the gun?" Dodo asked.

Rupert read on. "No. But they are testing the bullet to see what caliber it was."

"*You* must know a lot about guns," she said, tentatively. "Having been a soldier."

Rupert had entered the fray of WWI near the end of hostilities. He had been spared most of the dreadful fighting conditions and had been responsible for trying to save the war horses from destruction after their usefulness had passed. In spite of that, he did not like to dwell on his experience, and she broached the topic with a certain degree of caution.

As she watched, his face paled and she felt instant regret. "Yes. Too bally much. We all had a service pistol and then for actual warfare, we had rifles. Thankfully, I never had to use them." He paused, staring down memory's dark alley. "Lonnie was shot with some kind of pistol."

"See, that's more than I know. My knowledge stops at shotguns for hunting." She tapped her spoon on the table. "Do you want to go back to the scene and see if *we* can find the gun?"

"You really think it's worth it? If it were me, I'd have thrown it in the Thames."

"But it wasn't you. Perhaps it was valuable and they kept it. Or stashed it in a safe place to retrieve later."

"Your mind!" He scraped the dish to get all of the creamy remains.

"You love it!" she said with a wink. "What do you say?"

Rupert sighed. "I don't have any other plans tomorrow, so why not?"

As he examined the last vestiges of the crème in the glass jar, Dodo remarked. "I believe Americans carry handguns."

"That is a sweeping generalization!"

"Well, not all of them, of course, but I believe the right to bear arms is written into their constitution."

Rupert brushed her button nose with his finger. "I believe you are correct about that, darling."

"This is my first murder involving a gun, and Americans are on the suspect list. The logical thing would be to ask them if they carry weapons with them."

The waitress came with the bill, dressed in a starched, white apron over a modest, black dress with lace headband.

Rupert dropped his voice as she walked away. "Are you accusing a member of Smokey Syncopation of the crime?" Rupert asked.

"Not really. But don't you see, it might mean there was a gun in the vicinity last night. If they did not secure it well, someone could have stolen the gun and committed the crime. It's not like they're readily available here."

Rupert kissed the tips of her fingers. "Excellent point."

"So, we can look for a discarded gun at the site and later ask the Americans if they carry one."

"What if I just wanted to relax after a stressful event and go and watch some cricket?"

"Oh no, darling! You'd much rather spend time with me looking for guns, wouldn't you?"

Chapter 9

In the daytime, the Isle of Dogs appeared dramatically less romantic. Dodo was more than a little surprised that a huge, larger-than-life tall ship was docked at the end of Ferry Street, its tall network of masts and rigging towering over the tiny workers cottages like some giant ogre. It had been completely invisible at night. And there was activity and noise everywhere as the other warehouses were open for business, hundreds of men hauling cargo from ships in the dock. As for the odor, it had not improved. Dodo retrieved the handkerchief doused with lavender water she had packed in her clutch bag.

The derelict building itself looked far less appealing in the cold light of day. The sense of eeriness she had experienced two nights before, no more than a whisper of a memory. All police presence, and 'bright young things' removed, the warehouse sat quiet amidst the surrounding industry, like a forgotten, toothless, old widow.

Together, they walked to the spot where the body had been found behind the *Savoy* van. The dark stain of blood was all that remained of Lonnie Chapman. Dodo ambled over to where she had found the pile of Gauloises cigarettes, but they were gone, removed by the bevy of constables. She leaned against the wall where the pile of butts had laid, looking in the direction of the van and the side door she and Didi had entered. The spot gave a perfect, hidden view of both.

"From here the killer would be able to hide in the shadows and see everyone that came out of this side door. Keeping quiet until Lonnie had gone behind the truck, the killer could have struck while Lonnie was distracted by lighting his own cigarette. Essentially, he was a sitting duck." She walked as if going round the truck then cocked her finger as if it were a gun. "Two things spring to mind. One, the bouncer that guarded this side door, the hefty, bald chap rippling with muscles. I wonder if he saw or heard anything. The music was pretty loud so the gunshot may have been muffled. I'd like to talk to him. Two, the murderer must have known Lonnie was here on the Isle of Dogs performing and that he would smoke during their break. So, unless it was an assassin, it was someone who knew Lonnie, which is a problem since, according to Lucille, they only arrived in the country a few days ago. So that points to a band member as the murderer. Three, I'd like to know who else left the Green Room during the break."

The ground was a mix of dirt and gravel. Not a good mixture for footprints, and anyway, the catering staff would have been in and out of the door during the night.

"Shall we go inside?"

They entered through the side door and Dodo was amazed at the derelict aura of the stark interior without the lights, bodies and music.

"How do you choose the places?" she asked, knowing that Rupert never used the same venue twice.

"It's actually a bit of a game," explained Rupert. "I drive around areas of London I don't know as well and just tootle around until I see something that interests me. Then I ask about the availability of the deserted buildings through an intermediary. The owners are more than happy to do business with me when they see my offer for the evening rental. After all, the buildings are sitting doing nothing. I arrange for the electricity to be turned on for twenty-four hours and promise to leave the area as I found it." He put his hands in the pockets of his wheat-colored, baggy trousers. "You may have noticed, this one is actually not far from Limehouse." They had worked on a difficult case together in Limehouse the year before.

"No, I didn't, but it makes sense, as we're near the Thames."

The Isle of Dogs' heyday dated from the early 1800s when it was decided that London needed more docks. Narrow channels leading from the main river and guarded by gates were created. These gates could be closed at night to prevent thieves from stealing the cargo. The channels led to huge, manmade docks with large warehouses surrounding them. By the middle of the 19th century, every inch of the new docklands was dedicated to industry. Cottages were built for the dock workers and their families behind the warehouses. Since those times, its popularity had waned, but it still housed a lively, bustling community with several pubs and a fire station.

Dodo's heels echoed in the tall, empty space as she walked across the floor to the former Green Room. The curtain that hid the door had been removed. She pushed open the door that resembled a blemish in the whitish wall. With no window and no temporary lights, the room was almost pitch black.

"Do you have a torch, Rupert?"

"I might have one in the car. Hold on!" He ran back outside, the light from the open door not quite reaching the back corners of the room.

On his return, Rupert brandished the beam.

"Jolly good!" said Dodo with a smile. "You keep the door open to let in as much natural light as possible and I'll use the torch for the nooks and crannies."

The square room was empty of any furniture. She passed the ray of light across the floor then along the walls. Cobwebs and petrified spiders decorated the edges for the most part. However, in the far, right corner, something glinted. It was a gold tube of lipstick. Red. She put it in her pocket. The other corners were bare except for dust balls and some blue feathers she recognized from Miranda's boa. She retraced her footsteps to the middle of the room, sweeping the beam more slowly. As she did so, something else caught her eye. Crouching to the floor, she put her fingers out. It was a reed. The kind used for a saxophone. It went into her bag.

Continuing her search with the light, she slowed and almost missed a tiny brush used to clean the mouthpiece of a trumpet, since it was camouflaged by the dark floor.

"Look here!" said Rupert.

She swung the shaft of light around and saw that Rupert had something trapped under his shoe. He bent to pick it up. "Part of a dirty ticket for passage on the *Princess Charlotte*. Steerage. Must be old. Lucille and her crew would have been in first class."

Dodo wrinkled her nose. It was a grubby ticket and showed some water stains. She reached for the paper, turning it over to see if it showed a date. A partial, blue, ink stamp cut off the year, but the date was June 5th.

"Probably nothing, but I'll put it in my bag. You never know."

She snapped off the torch and stepped back into the main area.

A noise caught their attention and they locked eyes. "A bird?" suggested Rupert. "The windows up top are in bad shape." They waited, senses on high alert.

Rustle. Squeak.

A dark mouse ran across the floor and Dodo let out a shriek. Rupert laughed. "You wouldn't have done well as a soldier. There were rodents everywhere. I'll shoo it out."

"Oy!"

Chapter 10

Dodo and Rupert whipped around, coming face to face with a small ragamuffin of about ten. His shoes had holes bigger than Piccadilly Circus and his face was covered with several layers of grime.

"And who might you be?" asked Dodo, turning on the charm.

Bright, blue eyes shone out from the dirty skin as he took in Dodo's face. "I-I'm Willie."

"How do you do, Willie?"

A bashful smile touched his lips.

"Do you have a last name?" she asked.

He ran a dirty sleeve under his nose. "Nope." Whether he did or not, it was plain to see that he was not about to divulge it.

"What'choo doin' 'ere?" he asked.

"Do you remember a big party on Saturday night?" asked Dodo.

"'Cor, yeah!" he exclaimed. "I spent 'alf the night watchin' all the toffs arrivin'. Was you there?"

"We were. We've come back to look for something."

The eyes that had relaxed, tightened. "Is this about the dead fella?"

Dodo glanced at Rupert, holding her breath. "Sort of. Did you see anything?"

He screwed up his filthy nose. "Nah! It was too dark."

"Did you hear anything?" asked Rupert.

A slippery life on the streets shone from his sharp features. "Maybe I did. Maybe I didn't."

Rupert fished in his pocket for a sixpence and held it out. "I'm sure your time is very valuable."

Wary eyes fixed on the coin, then lurched between Rupert and Dodo as if Rupert were springing a trap.

"You can trust him," assured Dodo. She could see a tendril of decision, fine as the silk web of a spider, forming in the boy's mind as he considered the pair of them.

He lifted his pointed little chin. "That your car? The green one? Outside?"

"It is." Rupert took a step forward. "Would you like a ride?"

Here was a temptation the little urchin could not resist. "Really?"

"Of course."

"You take me for a ride and then I'll see what I can do for ya." The art of negotiation was well developed in the child, though if Dodo were his mother, she would frown on him taking rides from strangers even if they were well dressed. Then it occurred to her that he might not have a mother.

Willie followed them outside, sighing at the sight of the Lafayette, green roadster shining in the sunlight. "She's a smasher! Is it new?"

"I got her last year," responded Rupert.

The urchin put his hand out reverently and stroked the wheel hub as though it were a champion racehorse.

"There's a jump seat in the back. Hop on up and I'll take you for a spin."

Willie's spindly legs scrambled up and over the doors, and Dodo looked to see if Rupert was wincing, but instead he was smiling broadly. They slid into the front seats and Rupert pressed the starter. As the engine leapt to life, the little boy whooped and hollered with pure joy, his enthusiasm contagious.

Rupert pulled out of the yard and onto busy Harbor Street, swinging the sleek car away from the river. Willie kept punching the air and laughing like a sailor on leave as Rupert made a sedate path down the street past the fire station and the Lord Nelson pub. The king himself could not have been happier, and Willie waved at every passer-by, leaving them open-mouthed.

After a turn around the block, Willie asked, "Can it go any faster?"

Rupert accelerated sharply and Willie fell back, giggling with glee. "Wee!" he cried as they sailed past chatting mothers with babies on their hips and boys playing football in the street.

"This is the best day of my life," Willie screeched. Dodo couldn't help smiling.

Seeing a confectioner's, Rupert pulled to the curb. "Fancy some sweets, Willie?"

"Are you 'aving me on?" His little eyes narrowed with suspicion.

"I think you deserve some. Come on!" cried Rupert, already making for the shop door.

If Willie had harbored reservations before, they melted away like the morning dew, and he barreled out of the back of the car.

The tiny bell over the sweet shop door rang out, and a squat woman with a scarf covering a head full of curlers appeared through a screen.

Her eyes registered shock as they swung from Dodo and Rupert back to unkempt Willie.

"Master William here would like some sweets," said Rupert as Willie stared through the glass like Aladdin in the den of thieves.

"Right you are," replied the woman.

Rows and rows of glass jars containing colorful, sugary sweets stood like soldiers on shelves behind her.

"'Ow about, some pear drops and bull's eyes?" he said after a lengthy inspection of the store's wares.

The little shopkeeper pulled out some steps and reached up for the tall container. Unscrewing the lid, she poured pear drops into the scales as Willie watched her every move while licking his lips.

"Four ounces?" She cocked her eye and her tone simultaneously.

"Perfect!" Rupert replied.

Tipping the pear drops into a white paper bag, she expertly twirled it between her fingers and laid the treasure on the glass counter. She then repeated the process for the bull's eyes.

Rupert handed both bags to Willie, who looked like Christmas had come early as he stashed the bags in the pockets of his threadbare jacket.

Then Rupert handed the shopkeeper some coins, and they both followed Willie back out into the sunshine.

"Aren't you going to have one?" Dodo asked.

"I'm going to wait and share 'em with me mate, Charlie," he replied seriously.

"Ready for the return journey?" Rupert asked.

"You bet!" Willie hastened back to his perch on the jump seat.

Rupert took a more sedate pace back to the abandoned building, but Willie's shouts were just as enthusiastic as ever.

"Can we drop you off at home?" Dodo asked.

It was the wrong thing to say, and a brick wall rose up between them. "'Ere's good enough," said Willie.

"You said you might have heard something at the party," she prompted.

With hands cradling his laden pockets, Willie's eyes lit up. "I was watchin' the comin's and goin's at the front, and then it slowed down, so I was tryin' to kip 'round the back when I 'eard a weird popping noise. Got me wondering. I ran round to the side of the buildin' and that's when I saw 'im. And all the blood."

Dodo's attention roared to life. "You heard the gun?"

"Didn't sound like no gun, but 'e was bleeding. Must a been one, eh?"

"Did you see who fired it?"

69

"Nah. 'E'd already scarpered."

Drat!

"Did you see *anyone?*"

"I saw the lady what sings. Ya' know. The lady with dark skin and the pretty lips. But she weren't near the dead bloke. She was just lookin' at the stars and gettin' a bit o' fresh air. Didn't even know 'e was laying there bleeding. I was frozen scared to the spot."

Why had Lucille not told them she had gone outside?

"Then that skinny bloke came out to get somethin' from the van and I thought 'e was goin' to be sick all over the ground. 'E wailed like a girl and ran back inside. That's when I went to 'ave a butcher's at the body."

Dodo inwardly grinned at the casual use of the cockney phrase that was so much a part of the child's everyday language.

"That was exceptionally brave of you! And what did you see?"

"Saw that old geezer, dead as a doormat with blood oozing from 'is chest. But 'is eyes were open and I got spooked, so I ran back to the shadows and watched. I saw *you* come out." He looked at Rupert.

So, he did recognize them.

"Then I 'eard a noise behind me and 'igh-tailed it out o' there," Willie continued.

"Before the odd noise, did you hear anyone talking?"

Willie paused and Dodo looked at his bulging pockets. "It might not o' been 'im, but I thought I 'eard him say in a funny accent, 'What are you doing 'ere?', but I was 'alf asleep by then. You types keep late hours. But that *pop* woke me right up."

"Where were you sleeping, exactly?" she asked.

He pointed to some bushes near the back of the building. Close enough to hear what was going on in the alley.

"Soon as the police arrived, I scarpered," he admitted.

"Thank you, Willie. You've certainly earned your sweets. If we need to talk to you again, where can we find you?"

"You bring that green beauty 'ere an' I'll find *you*!" he declared with a wink and a wipe of his snotty nose. "Now, I'd best be getting back." He saluted, turned on his heel and disappeared through the bushes.

"Just when you think you've seen it all," Dodo laughed as they hopped back into the roadster.

Chapter 11

Rupert's new townhome gleamed like a shiny penny—on the outside. Dodo knew that the inside was another story. He had purchased the house after it was lost in a gambling scheme during their last case. It was a traditional London townhouse that had been the special home to generations of noble women, and its décor screamed the fact. The first thing Rupert had done was to employ a crew to strip all the floral wallpaper and paint the walls. Ernest Scott, his new valet and fiancée of Dodo's maid, Lizzie, was in residence to oversee the workmen.

Because of the chaos, Rupert was still residing at the mews house his uncle had left him until the townhouse was habitable.

"Hello!" he cried over the noise of the workmen. "Hello!"

Ernie's head appeared from a door at the end of the corridor. "Mr. Danforth! Were we expecting you?"

Rupert and Dodo edged past the painters. "No, no," Rupert assured him. "I just wanted to show Dodo the progress."

"Can I be of any assistance?" Ernie asked.

"No. Don't need to bother you. I'll show Dodo around. We'll come and see you in the kitchen before we leave."

"Then I'll put the kettle on and send round to the bakery for some sandwiches."

"Excellent!"

Dodo and Rupert retraced their steps into the industrious vestibule, and taking her hand, Rupert guided her up the stairs that were covered with a variety of drop cloths. A large chandelier hung from the center of the foyer draped in a cloth like a bride wearing a heavy veil.

At the top of the stairs, a pair of double doors opened onto a large drawing room with sash windows that overlooked the long back garden. Once-fussy walls were now a bare white, as were the old window frames. An enormous, Rococo Revival ceiling medallion dominated the room and Dodo could imagine the gorgeous chandelier that would eventually hang from its middle. Detailed crown molding framed the ceiling and matched the ornate fireplace mantle. The long windows that flanked the fireplace let in the welcoming afternoon sun.

It was right up Dodo's alley, clean and modern which a dash of antiquity.

"I thought I'd go with white everywhere in here. It's fresh, simple and chic."

"It's perfect!" declared Dodo. "All the light lifts my mood."

"It had awful flocked, purple wallpaper before. Horrid!" declared Rupert. "Depressed me every time I came in."

She could imagine modern black-and-white furniture centered around the fireplace and black, lacquer sideboards to contrast with the white walls. It would be the latest style.

"Come and see the rest."

They poked their heads into the first bedroom where great blooms of wallpaper fell from the walls and kissed the floor as workmen tried to scrape it off in large sheets. The old palette was light blue and pink. Dodo shuddered. "What color will you paint it?"

"What do you think about peacock blue with gold accents?"

'Fabulous!" she agreed.

The second bedroom was a little smaller and the walls had already been stripped bare. "I thought jade green for this one."

"Smashing."

Another set of double doors revealed the large main bedroom. It shared a twin ceiling medallion with the drawing room. This room had not been touched and was still adorned in rose petal wallpaper. It reminded Dodo of her grandmother's bedroom. Large windows on either side of a fireplace sat opposite where a canopied bed would reside.

"What are the plans for here?" she asked, feeling a pinch of awkwardness. Rupert had hinted at marriage several times but had not popped the question.

Rupert took a moment to answer, and she switched her gaze from the gaudy walls to his face. "I don't know. Thought I'd ask the most sophisticated girl I know for advice."

Dodo relaxed and clapped her hands. "Really? Oh, Rupert, I can do some research and plan something totally serene and soothing."

"That's my girl." He took her hand again. "Follow me." They entered an Edwardian dressing room, full of wall-to-wall, dark wood. "I'm going to rip all this out and make a bathroom since this house only has a shared one at the end of the hall."

"A bathroom that connects to the bedroom?" Dodo said aghast. "Whatever for? Won't it make the bedroom damp?"

"The bathroom will have a window for ventilation, and if you keep the door closed, the moisture from the bath shouldn't travel into the sleeping area."

Dodo wrinkled her nose. "It seems such a strange idea. Bathrooms are supposed to be removed from the sleeping quarters for hygiene purposes."

"So, you don't think it's a good idea?" Rupert asked, a shadow of disappointment clouding his brow.

"It's terribly innovative, but I'm not sure how it will work in practice," she reasoned.

"It's not set in stone yet. I wanted to run it by you first."

"Let me think about it," she said, spinning around in the dressing room.

"No hurry. There's plenty of work to keep the men occupied for a while yet."

Eventually, Rupert had shown her everything, and they ran down the basement stairs to the kitchen where Ernie was waiting, a tea pot brewing, filling the air with its familiar, comforting aroma.

Nothing had been touched down here. A large, oak table dominated the servants' eating quarters, and a wide, open fireplace with cast iron roasting hooks, long since cold, took up most of the back wall of the kitchen. More modern cast iron ovens lined the opposite wall and a large sink and draining board looked out a window that opened onto the long back garden.

"How is Lizzie?" Rupert asked Ernie.

"Tickety-boo! We're meeting up to see a matinée on my afternoon off."

"I don't know how you live in all this bedlam," remarked Dodo.

"Well, the kitchen is untouched as yet, and there is a butler's parlor that is still intact. My bedroom upstairs was the first room to receive any attention, and Mr. Danforth let me decorate it according to my own style. So, you see, I have my sanctuaries."

"How are the workers? Do they respect your authority?" Rupert asked.

"They do…but if I wasn't here jockeying them along, no work would get done, sir."

"I feared as much. That's why I asked you to move in right away. I'd like to get it all finished by Christmas. Then I can have a jolly housewarming party."

"That may be a little optimistic, sir," said Ernie, pouring them both a cup of tea.

"Then I'm counting on you to keep them all on track," said Rupert, grabbing a ham and pickle sandwich.

"Will you be staying for dinner, sir?"

"No, no. We have plans to have dinner with Miss Lucille Bassett and her remaining bandmates."

"I read about all that in the paper. What a tragedy!" declared Ernest. "I assume they will cancel all their British tour dates due to the funeral. I wonder if the deceased's family will come over and where it will be held?"

These were all very practical matters that a valet would consider, details that had not crossed Dodo's mind. "No doubt we will find out the answer to these questions this evening, Ernie. Are you a fan?"

"Oh, yes! Lizzie and I just bought some of their records, and I invested in a gramophone player for my butler's sitting room. But it is Miss Bassett's voice that gives the band its distinction, though I don't doubt the other members are great musicians in their own right." He stirred a sugar into his cup. "How does one go about auditioning for a replacement of such an iconic jazz band?"

Dodo and Rupert arrived early at Le Sous Sol, one of the best French restaurants in the city. But more than that, it was discreet, and quiet—perfect for celebrities in mourning. They secured the table in a secluded alcove and asked that their guests be seated upon their arrival.

"What were those questions you thought of when we were at the warehouse?" Rupert asked.

Elbows on the table, Dodo rested her chin on her hands. "I want to question your security fellow, the one at the side door all night. I assume you know how to contact him?"

"I can manage it," he said.

"I also want to ask the band members if any of them left the Green Room during their break. Especially after what Willie told us about seeing Lucille outside. And I want to know if this was really Lonnie's first trip to England or if he knew anyone here from a previous visit. Oh, and how they got here. Was it on the *Princess Charlotte*? I'm hoping

76

we can get a feel for how the band members felt about each other too."

"That's a pretty tall order for one dinner."

"I thought by now you knew that I'm a pretty exacting woman."

Rupert leaned over to kiss her gently as a shadow fell across the table.

Chapter 12

"Are we interrupting something?" The soft, waterfall cadence of the Louisiana deep south washed over Rupert and Dodo, their lips curving into smiles as they touched.

"Excuse us, Miss Bassett," said Dodo, pulling back from Rupert. "Please take a seat."

Lucille Bassett's generous lips curved into a bittersweet smile of their own. "Lulu, darlin'. My friends call me Lulu."

Dex and Cy were right behind her and slid into the seats beside them with knowing smiles.

"How are you all doing?" asked Dodo.

"If you mean, how are we after one of our best friends in the world is killed in your country? I've been better. This is not the welcome I expected." Lucille's stinging rebuke was evidence that she was having trouble keeping her anger at bay. And with good reason.

"It is terribly shocking," agreed Dodo. "Have the police made any progress?"

"I know we are colorful characters in the Deep South, but I want to pinch that man to make him react. I never met someone so expressionless and dry. He would burn into a fireball in the heat of the South."

Dodo pursed her lips fearing that their guests were in no mood for levity. Cy and Dex were letting Lucille do the talking, but their expressions were shouting agreement.

"When they told me the British were reserved, I underestimated the extremity," Lucille continued. "But to answer your question, he asked to interview us again and treated us as though *we* had killed our dear friend. I left feeling mighty fired up at him, I can tell you. To suggest that I would kill my Daddy's best friend, my own mentor, well, I had to ask the sweet Lord for forgiveness for the names I called him in my head."

"I am sure the inspector meant no insult," said Rupert. "But if you would like to take a more active role in finding out who did this to Lonnie, you should know that Dodo has quite the reputation as a—what do you call it in America? A gumshoe."

The liquid, ebony eyes snapped to Dodo, and with an upturned palm, Lucille pointed. "This pretty little thing is a detective?"

"I am," confirmed Dodo.

"Well, knock me down with a feather! How many cases you worked on?"

"At least nine," Dodo replied.

"And you solved every one of them?"

"Every one!"

"Girl, being around you is dangerous!" It was a barb that hit a little too close to home.

"So, what do you think?" asked Rupert.

"You're hired. I have no faith in this English copper. I'll pay any amount," responded Lucille.

Dodo held up both hands. "Oh, I don't charge for my services."

"What kind of numbskull business plan is that?" asked Cy, his droopy eyes perking up.

"It's more of a hobby," Dodo explained.

A waiter appeared with a white, linen tea towel over his arm, pencil poised over a notepad. Lucille brushed him away. "I haven't even looked over the menu yet. Can you give us a few minutes, honey?"

Silently, the waiter bowed and withdrew backwards as though he were at an audience with the king.

"I get a kick out of so many things here," sighed Lucille. "But your country killed my friend, and I can't forgive it."

"I can certainly see how that would taint your opinion of Old Blighty," said Rupert.

"Ole what now?" asked Dex, spreading out his palms.

"It's a nickname for Great Britain," Rupert explained.

Lucille shook her head. "They tell me we speak the same language, but I'm beginning to wonder."

For the next five minutes, Rupert and Dodo explained the French menu to the three Americans, and Rupert beckoned the waiter back.

"Did you enjoy the crossing?" asked Dodo to get the ball rolling in the right direction.

"It was a beautiful ocean liner," said Lucille. "We *had* booked passage on the *Voyager* but it got damaged, and after the Titanic disaster I didn't trust it, so we switched to the *Princess Charlotte.* I have never experienced that kind of luxury on a boat, and I thought the paddle steamers on the Mississippi were fancy."

"How was the weather?" Dodo asked.

"We had one good storm that sent us all back to our cabins, but the rest of the journey was like a millpond," chuckled Dex. "And nothin' was too much for those stewards. White gloves and everythin'."

"And the food was good?" Dodo asked.

"First class! I was worried I'd not fit into any of my performance gowns," replied the singer.

"Do you travel with a maid?" Dodo asked, wondering if there were more people in the entourage.

"No! I remember where I began, honey, and I don't ever want to forget it. The day I hire a maid is the day all this success has gone to my head. Nuh-uh." She narrowed her eyes. "No offense."

"None taken," Dodo assured her.

"You didn't bring any staff at all?" asked Rupert incredulously.

"Not a one. I pay people to help me as I go, if I need it." She leaned forward and whispered, "I have thirteen wigs with me so I never have to worry about my hair."

"Genius!" Dodo did not travel lightly when they went abroad, but she thought that Lucille's baggage must be excessive.

"I actually keep my own hair very short. It's easier that way." She eyed Dodo's silky, black bob. "But I'll be adding one more wig to my collection."

"I'm flattered." Dodo cupped the bottom of her hair with a hand and pushed it up a little. "Did the rest of you enjoy the journey?"

"The seasickness was awful at first, but once that was past, I thoroughly enjoyed it," said Cy. Dodo put his age at around thirty. "They had a band on board, and they let me join them some nights, though their style was a little more sedate than I'm used to. And like Lulu said, we were spoiled like royalty. A man could get used to that."

Dodo swiveled her gaze to Dex.

He squeezed his eyes shut. "It's not my favorite way to travel. I have this foolish fear when I can't see land in any direction. I'm much happier on solid ground. But, I agree, the service *was* outstanding. And the food! Most nights I was fuller than a tick on a dog!"

"And what about Lonnie? Was he a good traveler?" Dodo asked.

Mention of his name was akin to pouring a potion of doom over the table. The cheerful mood swung way south.

"He was happy as a hog in mud," said Lucille with a catch in her voice. "He grew up around the ocean and loved it. He would walk the ship every day to keep his joints from seizing up and chat up the chamber maids. He got such a kick out of eating in the dining room with all the grand folks. His eyes would shine like a child's."

"He told me he really felt like he'd made it when he was able to cross the sea on such a fine vessel and not have to travel below decks," said Dex. "He was a simple fella at heart."

Several waiters appeared bearing shellfish dishes and eggs mimosa.

Cy rubbed his large hands.

They spoke of Louisiana during dinner, then Dodo's family and some of her cases. By the time dessert made an appearance they had downed three bottles of wine, and Dodo could tell their guests were well loosened up. She decided it was time to bring things back to the murder.

"The night of the party, did any of you go outside for a cigarette or anything during your break?" she asked.

Lucille stiffened. "I don't smoke. Makes me cough."

"Me neither. I can't stand it." Dodo tried hard to make her tone as non-threatening as possible.

Lucille seemed to relax again. "I feel like the whole world smokes these days. And it's an occupational hazard in my line of work."

"So, except for Lonnie, you all stayed in the Green Room during intermission?"

Lucille pointed a blood-red fingernail at her. "I see what you're doing," she said like a lioness ready to pounce. "You're starting your investigation already. Why begin with his best friends in the world? What do we have to gain by his death? Nothing! In fact, we've lost a critical member of the band. We will never sound the same." Her tone was dangerous.

Dodo held up both hands in surrender. "I'm not accusing anyone. The fact is, gathering information is vital for an investigator, and the more information you have the better. Some little thing that one person noticed can break a case wide open. For example, Lonnie went outside. Therefore, I want to know who knew and whether any of you may have joined him and seen something that might prove relevant though it didn't seem important at the time."

Lucille's body had taken on a fighting stance, elbows on the table, chin thrust forward. But now she pulled back into her chair, nodding. "I see what you mean. I apologize. The loss of Lonnie has me all riled up."

"We were all in the Green Room enjoying the food, but there were no windows, and it was stuffy," offered Dex. "Lonnie pulled on a hat to hide his face and told us he was going to get a little fresh air. I said I'd join him. But before he could get out, this crazy, little lady grabbed him by the lapels and planted a kiss on him. Made me laugh. When we got out the side door, I was knocked back by that smell and changed my mind. Besides, I wanted to clean my sax between sets.

"When I got back, the room was empty. I opened my case and started pulling the mouthpiece off to wipe things down with my special cloth. A few minutes later, Lulu came in, humming to herself, and then Cy slipped in and sat in a chair, drumming his fingers on the arm."

So, they all left the room.

"Did you replace your reed?" Rupert asked.

"Why, yes!" exclaimed Dex. "Do you play?"

"No, but I'm familiar with that aspect," Rupert explained. "Do you keep the used ones?"

"Nah. I just throws them on the floor," Dex answered. "Little thing like that—no one's gonna care."

"Did any of you think it strange that Lonnie hadn't returned by the time you got back on stage?" Dodo asked.

"No," replied Lucille. "That man loved his smokes, and he didn't like to be hurried. The band would often start up after a break without him. He'd slip on stage when he was good and ready and just start playing. He said he was too old to hurry and too stubborn to be rushed at his age."

"How old was he?" asked Rupert.

"Fifty-eight and a half," replied Lucille. "Five years younger than my Daddy."

Dodo fixed her eyes on Cy. "Where did *you* go?"

"I slipped around the edges of the room, watching folks having a good time and enjoying the music. For white folks, that Crazy Train has great rhythm. I was surprised. Intrigued. Plus, I thought there was a door on the other side of the room, but by the time I realized that the only doors were the main entrance and the side door where the food was brought in, it was time to get ready for the next set."

"So, you left the Green Room but never left the building?" she confirmed.

"That is correct, little lady."

Lucille cocked a brow and threw a sidelong glance at Dex. "Well, now you know *I* left the room. I just wanted a breath of fresh air for my pipes before I had to go back on stage, but like Dex said, that air wasn't too fresh. I didn't see Lonnie—"

"He was behind the Savoy truck," Dodo explained.

Lucille's brow rippled. "That would explain it then. That bristling fella let me out and I just looked at the stars, marveling that I could see the same constellations as at home. I took a couple of deep breaths. But I must confess, the smell got to me too and I went back inside. Dex was there polishing his sax, and then Cy reappeared just minutes before we heard the backup band wrapping up."

"Had Lonnie been to England before?" Dodo asked.

"That man had barely left N'Orleans," chuckled Dex, running a hand over his short, dark hair.

"That's right," said Lucille. "We only go on tour once a year because Lonnie don't like to be too far from home. I had to work on him for a long time when we were invited to play here in London. Told him it would be the chance of a lifetime—" Her voice cracked.

Dodo reached out and placed her hand over the singer's.

"If I-I hadn't p-pushed him, he'd be alive," she sobbed, reaching for a handkerchief in her little shell-shaped handbag.

Dodo could not contradict Lucille's conclusion. Better to steer the conversation away from the sad realization. She reached into her own handbag and pulled out the lipstick tube, placing it on the table.

"I've been looking for that," said Lucille through wet lashes. "Where'd you find it?"

"It was in the Green Room. We went back to do a little snooping."

Though tempted to reveal that there was a young witness to the events of the evening, Dodo had no desire to put Willie in any danger. Nothing said tonight had set her sixth sense tingling, but it was early days yet, and she could not rule out any of the band members from the deadly deed. She needed more background.

Lucille reached for the tube, pulled a matching gold mirror from her handbag and touched up her lips, pursing them to even out the lipstick and then pouting.

"Was Lonnie married?"

"Once. A long time ago," said Lucille. "It ended badly. She ran off with one of his friends."

"And there was no special lady since?" pushed Dodo.

"That woman shattered his heart into a million pieces. He had no desire to put himself through that again. He was married to the piano."

"No children?"

"No kids. He treated me like the daughter he never had." A single tear tracked down Lucille's cheek.

Chapter 13

Logic told Dodo that the most likely people to have had a hand in Lonnie's demise were the performers, though she hadn't yet figured out how anyone on stage at the time could have done it. Having questioned the surviving members of Smokey Syncopation she was now determined to mine Crazy Train for information and had called to invite them on a lazy trip down the river, a trip that would take them right past the Isle of Dogs.

As Dodo and Rupert approached the dock near Westminster, where they had arranged to meet the band, she almost didn't recognize Miranda in the small crowd. Today, her hair was mouse brown and worn in a short bob under her hat, and she was wearing far less makeup. Honestly, if Gerry and Fred had not been with her, Dodo might have walked straight by.

"Hello!" said Miranda touching her hair and smoothing the understated, lavender frock. "Thought I'd come as myself today. Plain old Edna."

"Just as lovely," said Rupert, which, as usual, was just the right thing to say.

Gerry and Fred were dressed casually in tan trousers and cream jackets, and both raised their straw hats in greeting.

A white pleasure boat pulled in to the bottom of the stairs, and a swarthy sailor type called up, "Danforth?"

Rupert raised a hand. "That's us."

He helped Dodo and Miranda down the mossy steps, and the two women settled into comfortable seats in the rear of the luxury craft.

Miranda giggled. "I've been to London before, but I've never done anything like this."

"It's my favorite way to see the city on a sunny day," said Dodo as the boat rocked gently while the men found their seats.

Gulls dipped for fish and screamed into the bright, cloudless sky with their prey. Other pleasure boats whipped by, the wake making their own boat rock harder. Miranda gripped the side.

"You've been to London before, then?" Dodo asked.

"Oh, yeah. A couple of times but before I had any of my own money. Took the bus or tube everywhere. Did the touristy things, you know?"

"What was your favorite?" asked Rupert, turning around.

"The Tower," she said without hesitation. "Gave me shivers to be in something so old."

"We'll pass it today," said Dodo with satisfaction. "You get a lovely view from the river."

"What about you two?" asked Rupert. "Have you ever been to the capital before?"

"Nah," said Gerry. "Not a great traveler, me. Never saw the point. But I'm enjoying this trip even though that copper is making us stick around because of the—well, you know." His lips twisted in emphasis.

"I barely had enough money to eat before all this," said Fred, his voice flat. "Never any money for a luxury like traveling."

It was at times like this that Dodo was grateful for the reminder that she lived a very privileged life. It was so easy to take these things for granted.

"How do you like it?" she asked him.

"To be honest, it's a bit crowded for my taste, and no one seems to understand me. But there are some interesting things." It wasn't a ringing endorsement.

Dodo turned back to Miranda. "How do you like the hotel? You're at *The Partridge*, aren't you?"

If Dodo hadn't been watching her, she would have missed the slight coloring of Miranda's cheek. "We were, but we moved to another one."

The unspoken message was that they had moved to a cheaper hotel since they were required to stay longer than they had planned. It implied that since the band were still on the path to fame, funds were probably tight. Dodo dropped the subject.

"Oh, look! You can just see the dome of St. Paul's."

All three heads swiveled in the direction Dodo pointed. The river was smooth and the weather perfect as the boat sliced through the chilly water.

"The Tower!" cried Miranda, almost jumping up but remembering just in time that she was in a boat. Tourists strolling along the cobblestones outside Traitor's Gate waved to the boats on the river. Miranda waved back.

"This is amazing! Thank you for inviting us," she said, beaming.

"It was the least we could do since you're stuck here," responded Dodo.

Fred was reaching his hand into the water, letting his fingers drag through the waves, and Gerry could not stop grinning as they passed under Tower Bridge.

"I've never been on a motorized boat," Fred cried.

As they took the bend in the river, Dodo wondered if their guests would recognize it as the place they had performed and where the murder had occurred. No one did. They swept past with Greenwich on the right. Rupert had made plans with the driver to turn around just past the area of the Prime Meridian and swing back along the south bank until they passed Westminster again, continuing their journey east through Kew and onto Hampton Court, home of the infamous King Henry VIII. There was a dear little riverside pub where they proposed to eat lunch.

With the wind in her hair and the sun in her eyes, it was easy for Dodo to briefly forget that something as dark as a murder had happened, but her motives for the outing were not all altruistic. Dodo had wanted time alone with the band members to determine if they had any connection to the dead musician other than meeting him the night of the performance.

"Have you traveled outside England at all?" she asked Miranda as they passed Kew Gardens Pier.

The slight frown indicated that Miranda was struggling with irritation. As though Dodo should know not to ask such a stupid question, but it was the only way to get to the answers Dodo needed.

"No. I've not had that pleasure," replied Miranda in a tight tone.

"When did you first hear Smokey Syncopation?" Dodo asked to lift the tension.

Miranda's scowl immediately transformed into whimsy. "It was about five years ago. Right at the end of the war. I was seventeen. My dad had the radio on in the kitchen and I was peeling potatoes. I dropped my peeler right then and pointed at the wireless. I told my dad that's what I wanted to sing. Smooth jazz. I can still remember him going over to the piano in the sitting room and trying out the chords."

A quick calculation put Miranda's current age at twenty-two; just one year older than Dodo. She wondered how old the rest of the band were.

"I 'member the first time I heard them," said Gerry. "I's walking past the local barber's shop and he had the radio on. Stopped me in my tracks. I never heard anything so smooth. Went right home to practice. Used a long brush to try to replicate the swishing sound on the drum. Tried it at a wedding and got a nice clip round the ear from the band leader. But I still practiced at home. When I heard Miranda and her dad at the pub, I knew that type of drumming was just what they needed to sound more professional."

"How about you, Fred?" asked Rupert.

Fred's unmemorable, sharp face folded into thought. "I'd say right after Mr. Smith took me on. He put one of their records on the gramophone and had me listen, then asked me to play it. Felt strange at first but I got used to it in time."

"They are my inspiration," admitted Miranda. "That's why it was such an honor to perform with them. Do you think Miss Bassett really liked my singing or was she just being nice to a beginner?"

"I think I can say without reservation that Miss Bassett was impressed. She doesn't seem the type to give out insincere compliments."

Miranda's whole face shone with a huge smile. "It's like a dream. If I can just get her endorsement by performing with them again, I think we'll hit the big time. Don't you, Gerry?"

Gerry waved a hand of assent in the air as the grand, orange castle, Hampton Court, came into view, and the boat pulled to a staircase below a pretty, brick pub with flowers in baskets hanging in a beer garden.

"Here we are," said Rupert as the boat bumped against the bank. He addressed the sailor. "We'll be back in two hours."

"Right you are, sir," replied the boat driver. "Gives me time to get something to eat myself."

The charming pub was as far removed from the working-class men's pubs of the inner city as mountains were from the ocean. The décor inside indicated a woman's touch. Flowers graced every surface, and instead of dark woods, the walls were whitewashed, and all the furniture was painted a glossy white. Couples occupied nearly every table.

They stepped back into the beer garden and found a table with five chairs in the shade of an enormous oak tree. It was perfect.

"Not like my pub back home," commented Gerry. "You can smell the stale beer on the floor a mile away." He laughed and it was as if a hippopotamus had walked in.

A young girl came to offer them menus, and after some deliberation and explanations, they each ordered a ploughman's lunch.

"What do you do for fun?" asked Rupert as they waited.

"I'm learning to read—words and music," said Fred. "Never saw the point before, but Miranda's dad told me they were good skills to have."

"Did you not go to school?" asked Dodo.

"Nope. My mam made me stay back to help with the babies. She said if I was going to work on the docks in Merseyside there was no point to learning."

"Where are your family now?" she asked.

"All but me and a brother died of dysentery in 1910, and we were left to fend for ourselves."

He said it with detached resignation, but Dodo felt like her shoe was wedged firmly in her mouth.

"I play polo," said Rupert in an attempt to save the conversation.

"What's that?" asked Gerry.

"It's a bit like croquet on horseback without the little goals. Just one big one."

Gerry cocked a brow. "Horseback?"

Rupert gave a quick rundown of the game to the incredulous pair. By the looks on their faces she guessed they did not approve.

"The Prince of Wales plays," said Rupert in a last-ditch effort to gain their favor. It didn't work.

"I knit," said Miranda. It gets cold in Liverpool, and it was a skill my mam had. I decided it would make me feel close to her."

"Are you any good?" asked Dodo, who had often admired Lizzie's handiwork.

"Nah! But I keep my dad stocked with hats." Miranda doubled over with laughter.

"I play dominos at the pub," said Gerry. "Passes the time and I win a few bob now and then."

"What about you?" Miranda asked Dodo.

"I dabble in fashion," she replied. "I'm an ambassador for the House of Dubois in Paris."

"That explains your dresses," said Miranda. "I'd kill for some of those."

The singer had a much fuller figure than Dodo. "How about I gift you a dress of your choice when you make it big?" she suggested.

"Really?"

"Yes, I mean it. It will be great advertising for the fashion house. I'd love to do it."

"That'd be grand," replied Miranda.

"What about your other hobby?" said Rupert. Everyone looked at him.

"You mean detecting?" Dodo asked.

"You're a detective? Who do *you* think killed Lonnie?" asked Miranda, her big, green eyes serious. "Was it just some random stranger hanging around the yard? If you'll excuse me saying so, Mr. Danforth, it wasn't the safest of areas."

Dodo looked into everyone's faces before answering. "It's really too early in the investigation to tell."

"Not a great introduction to Great Britain for the Americans, is it?" commented Miranda. "I hope it doesn't put Miss Bassett off returning. How's she doing? She suggested getting together again. I'd really like to do that."

"Lonnie was like a father to her. She's taking it hard," Dodo replied. "In fact, she's hired me to find his killer."

Chapter 14

Ronald Briggs was perhaps the tallest person Dodo had ever met. Leaning against a lamp post outside the Spotted Duck, brushing his trim mustache with a finger, Dodo nicknamed him Gulliver. His hatless, bald head simply emphasized the height that had been less obvious in the dark of the SJP.

"Hello, guv!" When God was handing out voices, Ronald must have been in the wrong spot and received the voice of a man who would stand only five feet four. She remembered wondering, briefly, at the surprising tenor pitch of his voice at the party, but the memory had disappeared into the abyss after the murder.

"Thanks for meeting us, Ronnie," said Rupert, looking up. "My boss wanted me to tie up some loose ends with the police."

"No problem, guv. When you're paid that handsomely you don't mind doing a little extra, if you know what I mean." He pushed a thumb against his nose and winked.

"Shall we?" said Rupert, indicating the door to the pub.

Rupert picked a fairly private, high bench seat in the back near a window. The middle of a weekday afternoon meant there were plenty of tables to choose from.

"What are you having?" he asked.

"Pineapple juice for me," said Dodo.

"Pint of best bitter," replied Ronnie.

"I'll be right back."

Dodo was left alone with the high-pitched giant.

"I understand you were in the army," Dodo began.

"Yes, miss. Ten years." The mustache stroking began again in earnest. "Started when I was eighteen as a regular, and then the war began, and for a bootneck like me, it was instant promotion."

Dodo clasped her hands on the black table. "I imagine you saw a lot of action."

"More than a man ever wants to see." He touched his head. "Made my hair fall out in great patches and its never grown back, so I started to shave it." He rewarded her with a unique side smile. "Saves a lot of time in the morning."

"I don't doubt it," she chuckled. "Do you have a family, Mr. Briggs?"

"No. The war messed with my head as well as my hair. Couldn't put a lady through that. No way!" Ronnie looked toward the bar and tipped his shiny crown. "What's he want anyway?"

Dodo jumped at the chance to talk about the night of the crime. "There were some discrepancies in what various people said about the party, and we just wanted to clear them up."

"I was interviewed by the police at the time and two days later." His small eyes became wary. "Am I under suspicion?"

"Oh no! Not at all." Dodo leaned forward and fluttered her eyelashes. "It's just that you were in the perfect spot to see people leave by the side door. We want to pick your brain."

Ronnie relaxed. "Oh. I was under strict instructions to only let a select group of people in and out that side door. How can I 'elp?"

"Actually, before we start, I should tell you that I'm an amateur sleuth and Smokey Syncopation have hired me to find who killed Lonnie Chapman."

The minute, coppery eyes widened in disbelief. "A looker like you, messing in crime? I can't believe it."

Rupert caught the tail end of the conversation and placed the three glasses on the table. "It's true, old chap. Beauty and brains."

Ronnie ran a calloused hand down his face. "Well, I never!"

Dodo jumped back in. "We went back to the warehouse in the daylight, and it struck me that every time you opened that door you had a clear view of the Savoy van and anyone around it. My conclusions lead me to suppose that the killer was waiting for Lonnie on the other side of the van in the shadows. Did you notice anyone hanging around out there?"

Before answering, Ronnie considered. "It was dark, and a couple of the waiters went out to the van to get things. I wasn't really looking for loiterers." He slapped his head. "I do remember looking out thinking I heard someone or felt someone watching, but it was just one time. Forgot all about it."

"Was that after you let Lonnie out or before?"

His lips twisted. "Before, I think."

Of course, he could have heard Willie, not the killer.

"Did you happen to smell anything like French cigarettes?"

"I did! Nasty things, those. I like Woodbines, myself. They were in our ration boxes in the war. Yeah, I remember wondering who was smoking those stinky French cigs, but it was a posh crowd so I just put it down to that." Ronnie took a long swig from his beer mug.

"Can I get you another?" asked Rupert.

"Don't mind if I do, guv," replied Ronnie.

As Rupert left to refill Ronnie's mug, Dodo asked, "We have a witness that says they saw Miss Bassett go outside for a bit, around the time of the murder. Do you remember her?"

"Hard not to! She's a woman you can't easily forget, and she has that pretty sing-song voice. She told me she needed to get some fresh air—not that the air round there was very fresh, mind you!" His laugh was a bit of a honk. It made Dodo smile.

"Do you remember the time she went out, by any chance?"

His upper lip pushed the mustache into his nostrils. "About ten minutes before they went back on, I'd say."

His statement corroborated what Lucille had said. Which meant Lonnie was probably already dead on the other side of the van.

The pub was beginning to fill up with flat-capped men.

"Did anyone unexpected come out that side door?" Dodo asked.

Ronnie shook his head. "I was under orders to direct people to the front doors unless it was a member of one of the bands, the staff, Mr. Danforth or you and your sister. Then there was that foppish bloke you brought out, but Mr. Danforth was with you, so I thought that was alright."

"And did Lonnie talk to you as he left?"

"Oh, yeah. Very friendly bloke. He asked my name and where I was from, then had a bit of a laugh about a girl who had tried to kiss him on his way out but missed. After that he walked around to the other side of the van, and I closed the door. I didn't hear no gunshot in case you're wondering."

"Well, the music *was* very loud, and people were shouting over it. It's not really a surprise."

"No, but I feel bad. Like I failed at my job. If I'd heard anything I might have been able to catch the killer."

Rupert returned. "You did a fine job. You kept that side door private. That's not always an easy thing to do."

Ronnie cradled the new pint. "I'd be happy to work for your boss any time in the future."

"I'll let him know, though he doesn't usually use the same team more than once."

Ronnie took a sip, the foam clinging to his mustache. "It's an interesting operation, if you don't mind me saying. Pays well too. What's your boss's name?"

"I'm sworn to secrecy," replied Rupert, miming pinching his lips together. "It's more than my job's worth to tell you."

96

Cynicism made a brief appearance on Ronnie's features. "Ah, well. I suppose the rich are entitled to their foibles." He checked the clock on the wall. "Well, if that's all, I must be going. Dropping in on my old mum for a spot of tea." He downed the rest of the pint in one swallow.

As they watched him lope through the tables that had filled even more while they were sitting, people couldn't help staring.

"Was he any help?" asked Rupert.

"He corroborated Lucille's timeline for going outside for a breather, but he didn't see anything else."

"He seems to be a reliable fellow, and his size is a distinct advantage. I might just consider making him my permanent head of security."

"I'd say that was a wise move," Dodo agreed.

They were now meeting the chap who had been the head of the wait staff for the SJP in the alley behind the *Savoy*. He had an afternoon break. As Dodo and Rupert approached, the waiter took a long drag on his cigarette, squinting his eyes against the smoke, and dropped the butt to the floor, crushing it under his shoe.

It struck Dodo that the smoker of the Gauloises cigarettes had not done that.

The young waiter, who had reminded Dodo of a butcher at the party, ran his palm down his shirt then held out a hand. "Mr. Danforth."

"Sam."

"You said you wanted to ask me some questions." A pinch of concern lingered at the corner of his eyes.

"That's right. Miss Bassett is not too satisfied with the speed of the police investigation into her friend's death, so we said we'd help out. La—Miss Dorchester here dabbles in detective work."

"Does she now?" said Sam, chewing his cheek and fingering his black hair. "Fire away. I've only got five more minutes."

"Were all the waiters known to you?" Dodo asked.

His face squashed into an apology. "Well, mostly. Some were friends of friends in the business."

"Were you satisfied with their work?" she continued.

"For the most part. One chap seemed to disappear from time to time but I was so busy I couldn't check up on him. I figured he'd gone for a smoke or something."

"Do you remember his name?" asked Dodo.

"Vlad something. He had an accent. Don't know his last name. I paid them all in cash after I got paid."

"Do you remember where he works?" she pushed.

He thought for a minute then snapped his fingers. "Cooper's in Bloomsbury. I've been there a couple of times. Thought it was a good reference." He raised worried eyes to Rupert. "Though I didn't actually check it out."

"Did you see or hear anything out of the ordinary that night?"

"I've been thinking hard about it since I talked to the police," he said, running a hand through dark brown hair. "I popped a bottle of champagne and thought I heard an echo. At the time I assumed it was because of the huge building, but now I wonder if it wasn't the gunshot I heard."

Here was something useful. Dodo took a step closer. "What time was that?"

"The redhead, Miranda, had been singing for about twenty minutes."

Dodo scribbled the time in her notebook.

"You know Miss Masters, don't you?" said Rupert, wagging a finger at Sam. "It was you who suggested she apply to be the backup band."

A tsunami of concern washed over his pale skin, and he could hardly look Rupert in the eye. "Yeah, she's my cousin. But she's not a suspect, is she?"

"Everyone is a suspect in the beginning of an inquiry," said Dodo.

"When I 'eard Mr. Danforth needed another band, I told her. Even though she's my cousin, she's pretty amazing."

"I can't disagree with that," conceded Rupert with a chuckle.

"Anything else odd happen that night?" Dodo persisted.

"I was run off my feet the whole time until the police came, and then everything came to a screeching halt. My mind was on keeping everything flowing. I've never been in charge of anything before and I didn't want to let Mr. Danforth down. But it was exhausting." With a sheepish grin he continued, "But I was honored to do it and I'd be happy to do it again. The money was more than I get paid in a month here."

"Sorry," said Rupert. "My boss has a policy of using fresh blood every time."

"Too bad! Well, if there's nothing else, I need to get going." He saluted and pushed through a swing door.

"What do you think?" Rupert asked Dodo as the young man hurried inside.

"I think we need to find this Vlad."

Chapter 15

Even a murder could not interrupt the normal demands and flow of everyday life, and Renée had returned to Beresford House for another wedding dress fitting with Didi. However, this time, instead of living in the moment with her sister, Dodo's mind was cluttered with the murder investigation.

She was convinced this was no random killing. Something in Lonnie's personal or professional life was the key to the motive. Another hurdle was that since Lonnie was an American, David, her usual source of background information, would be of no use. The only light was that the interview with Sam the waiter had given her a new lead. Vlad.

After a light lunch at a fashionable bistro by the Thames, she and Rupert made their way over to Cooper's restaurant in Bloomsbury, a district in the West End of town. It was a corner restaurant with a curved entrance painted in bright blue with decorative, white plaster moldings above the door.

They had carefully timed their visit between the lunch and dinner rush and the place was almost empty. A waiter looked up with a question on his face.

"I'm afraid we've just stopped serving lunch," he said, in a cockney accent masquerading as a posh one.

Coughing to cover a giggle, she explained, "Oh, we're just hear to speak to Vlad."

The ripples on the waiter's brow deepened. "Who?"

"Vlad. We were told he works here," said Dodo.

The waiter tipped his head, but the brilliantine in his hair ensured it did not move an inch. "I've worked here for ten years, and I can tell you we have never had a waiter here by the name of Vlad."

Dodo's spirits flagged. "Then we are mistaken. Do excuse us."

Outside on the pavement, Dodo shielded her face from the sun. "A wild goose chase! Who do you think was lying? Sam or the man who called himself Vlad?"

"I'd put my money on Vlad," replied Rupert. "Sam is eager to work for me again. He wouldn't risk that by lying."

"Good point. So, we have a man who disguises himself as a waiter to get into the SJP and then disappears when he should be working. I think Mr. Vlad, or whatever his *real* name is, has shot to the top of my suspect list."

"What better way to infiltrate a place and move about freely than wearing a waiter's uniform?" said Rupert. "No one would question him going out through the side door, not even Ronnie. But how on earth are we ever to find him? Fake name, fake references."

"We need to go back and ask Sam for a better description."

♪

Having called the Savoy, they discovered that Sam was working but that he had another break at four o'clock. They were waiting outside the back door.

"Sam!" called Rupert.

His face registered concern mingled with hope. "Mr. Danforth. What are you doing here again? Did your boss give the green light for me to work one of his parties again?"

"We're not here about that," Dodo explained. "We need to talk to Vlad. He lied to you. He has never worked at Cooper's."

A line formed between Sam's worried eyes, and he ran the back of his hand across his mouth. "That's what he told me. Said he'd been there for two years. Why would he lie?"

Why indeed?

"Did you say he was a friend of a friend? Can you remember who that friend was?" asked Dodo.

Sam looked up at the slice of sky visible in the alley. "Now that you mention it, I don't think he said the name of the friend. But it was for one night only, so I wasn't too picky." His head snapped back. "Are you saying he might be the murderer?"

"We're not saying anything conclusive at this point, but it is suspicious. Can you describe him in more detail? Did you say he had an accent?"

Sam grabbed his chin. "Yes. But whether it was Russian, Polish or Greek I wouldn't know. He definitely wasn't English."

"What did he look like?" she prodded.

Guilt paled Sam's face. "Uh, short, kind of stocky. He had really big muscles like a boxer or something. I should have paid more attention."

"What about his hair?"

Sam snapped his fingers. "Almost white blond. You don't see that much 'round here." He closed his eyes tight as if trying to conjure up the man's face in his mind. He punched the air. "He had a small scar in the corner of his right eye. Like he had fallen as a child. It dragged the eye down a little. Other than that, his face was kind of forgettable."

"That's good, Sam. Very good," said Dodo. "Do you have the names of the other waiters that evening? Maybe one of them got to know him better."

"I have the list in my locker if you don't mind waiting a moment."

Sam headed back inside as a fishmonger's van pulled up. Dodo and Rupert stepped aside while the driver unloaded cases of fresh sole and trout.

Sam returned, panting, and offered Dodo the paper which was crumpled and stained. There were ten names.

She sighed. It would take a lot of time to interview all of them.

"Sorry I couldn't be more help," Sam said, shuffling his feet. "I hope the fact that I didn't vet him better won't be a black mark against me, Mr. Danforth."

Rupert frowned. "Like I said, my boss never uses the same crew twice."

Sam hung his head and kicked the ground.

"But your description of the chap is helpful, and this list may prove invaluable," said Dodo, handing him her card. "If you think of anything else, could you give me a call?"

Sam looked at the card. "Lady?" His brows knitted, his face full of indecision. "I knew you was a toff, but if I've been disrespectful in any way, I apologize."

Dodo patted the air. "Think nothing of it. I didn't tell you I had a title for my own reasons. I had no expectations, I assure you."

Sam slid the card into the small pocket on the front of his waistcoat and touched his finger to his forehead. "If you'll excuse me, m'lady, I'm going to run and get some chips for my tea."

Rupert blew air through his teeth as Sam ran off. "Our best candidate looks like a dead end."

"Don't give up yet! Hopefully, Vlad revealed something more helpful to one of the other waiters."

"Rupert, you look done in!" cried Lady Guinevere when he and Dodo arrived at Beresford House for dinner.

"We have spent the last two days interviewing waiters—ouch!" Rupert bent down to rub his shin.

"For your little parties?" asked Guinevere

"Something like that," he murmured.

The truth was that Dodo and Rupert had interviewed all the waiters on Sam's list and come up empty handed. 'Vlad' had kept to himself, keeping his head down, doing the job until he disappeared briefly around the time of the murder, then vanishing into the sunset. The whole caper had been a complete waste of time. It was looking more and more like everything about Vlad was fabricated. Which made him the perfect suspect for an assassin. Too bad he had slipped through their fingers.

Which led to the deeper question; what had Lonnie done to warrant being taken out of the game by a professional?

She needed to talk to Lucille again.

The conversation around the Dorchester dinner table revolved around the upcoming nuptials, which was a far safer topic for Lady Guinevere's ears than the murder investigation.

"Renée said she's ready to fit you for your bridesmaid's gown. Can you be here in three days for that?" asked Didi, her eyes shining. "I've chosen lavender satin."

Pastels were not Dodo's favorite, but they were the obvious choice for her blonde-haired, peachy skinned sister. And Dodo knew she would like the style since she had helped Didi to choose the design of the bridesmaid's dress.

"I'll be there," she replied. "What time?"

"Around ten," Didi announced.

After dessert, Lady Guinevere excused herself. She was going to see a local review with a friend in the neighboring town. When the rest of them filed into the drawing room, Lord Alfred rubbed his hands together, eyebrows raised.

"So! The papers have been full of the murder at the jazz party, but they don't seem to have arrested anyone. How's your own investigation going?" Lord Alfred knew his daughter well enough to know she would be up to her elbows in sleuthing.

"It is looking more and more like—how do the novels put it? Like a 'hit' was put on Lonnie."

"I thought he was shot," responded her father.

"It means that the murderer paid someone else to kill him, Daddy," explained Didi.

He cocked a bushy brow. "A mercenary?"

"Yes, something like that," Dodo responded.

"Good grief! Does that make it harder to solve?" he asked.

Dodo bent her head to the side. "The short answer is yes. The longer answer is that it means we need to concentrate harder on motive. Who had a reason to want Lonnie dead? Who gained from his death? Those are hard things to discover when the victim is from a different country."

"You could always send a telegram to the police department in New Orleans. Or to the local newspaper office," suggested Didi. "If there were scandals involving Lonnie, they would have written about it because he was famous."

"Didi! That's brilliant! Why didn't I think of it?" cried Dodo.

Didi's bashful smile showed how much she appreciated her sister's compliment.

"What time is it in America?" asked Dodo.

"One in the afternoon in New York," said Rupert looking at the time. "But New Orleans is several time zones over, so it's probably closer to two or three."

"Perfect! Let's go!" She pulled Rupert to standing, dragged him out into the hall and pushed him into the telephone cabinet.

Having been put through to a telegraph office, she dictated a message for the biggest newspaper office in New Orleans, representing herself as a journalist.

Subject: Murder of Lonnie Chapman stop requesting clips of scandals in Lonnie's past stop send relevant headlines by telegraph at my expense to Beresford House, Herts stop

As she replaced the telephone earpiece, she beamed at Rupert. For the first time, she felt hopeful that when she awoke in the morning, she would have a real lead.

105

Bouncing into the breakfast room, Dodo's heart leaped when she saw an envelope by her plate. She ripped it open and read the telegram.

Several scandals stop girl claiming to be his daughter from affair stop dispute with Clay Bassett over club ownership stop claim of plagiarism stop credit Thomas Eldridge New Orleans Post

Eureka! Here was fodder for motives indeed.

As she re-read the missive, her mood deflated a little. Without the full stories, these headlines were of little practical use. She tapped the table then slapped her palm on the surface. Lucille must know about them. Especially the one about the club ownership dispute with her father.

It was now imperative that Dodo meet with the prickly singer again, and this time she would be walking on a tightrope.

Chapter 16

The invitation from Lucille Bassett for Rupert and Dodo to go to dinner with Smokey Syncopation and Crazy Train at the Ritz could not have come at a better time for her investigation. And as Dodo knew, the ambitious Miranda had been eager to get together with Lucille since the night of the murder.

Dodo was meeting Rupert at the restaurant since she had been fitted for the bridesmaid dress that afternoon, and Rupert had business in London and at his townhome. She had been busy fabricating the rest of the story behind those headlines from Louisiana all day long. Some of her ideas were utterly outrageous and made her consider writing fiction, but others seemed more likely. Just how close to the truth they were, she hoped to discover this evening.

Due to some roadwork on a bridge just outside of town, Dodo was a little late and found everyone already seated at the table in the Louis XVI style, pink, marble dining room. A quick glance around as she was seated revealed Douglas Fairbanks and Noel Coward at a table in one corner and Lady Cynthia Asquith with an entourage in another. As Dodo flicked her serviette and placed it over her blue, chiffon dress, she took a moment to marvel at the trompe l'oeil ceiling with its pink clouds.

Rupert reached for her hand.

"Isn't this fun!" squealed Miranda, the harsh sound clashing with the sophisticated décor. Dodo suspected that a restaurant like the Ritz was still out of her budget, but it wouldn't be long until she would be able to afford to dine at such places.

Miranda's thick, auburn wig was styled in large, Hollywood waves that clung to a neck decorated with a garish, but eye-catching, necklace. Her perfectly made-up eyes shone with nerves and childlike excitement. Dodo guessed she was banking on this dinner to cement future plans to play with Smokey Syncopation.

"This is quite some place you have here," said Lucille smoothly, indicating the room with her head. "I asked the concierge of our hotel for suggestions."

Truth be told, Dex and Cy and the other players from Crazy Train looked decidedly out of place in this temple of wealth and fame, and Dodo speculated the men were wishing the dinner had been at one of London's many famous pubs.

"I have never seen the like outside of New York City," Lucille continued.

"The architecture is a fusion of French and American styles," Rupert explained. That's probably why it looks familiar."

"And Buckingham Palace is just behind here at the top of Green Park," added Dodo.

"You don't say." Lucille took a sip of the golden liquid in her flute.

After ordering, Miranda launched into a speech about how honored they were to have been the supporting act for Smokey Syncopation, and would Lucille agree to them joining forces again while they were touring Britain?

Lucille sucked in her cheeks. "Though I am as impressed as the next person by ambition, I must say I find your request to be ill-timed, Miss Masters. I have just lost not only a key player and a dear friend, but our manager. Out of respect, I have canceled our scheduled appearances in this country." She flashed her enviably long, black eyelashes at Miranda. "I'm sure you understand."

Though the smooth southern tones disguised the directness of the message, Lucille's meaning was crystal clear, and Dodo swung her gaze to see how the slight was received by Miranda. Rather than looking abashed at her faux pas, Miranda was smiling broadly like an eager puppy.

"Of course, of course. I meant no offense. I just didn't want to look a gift horse in the mouth. You are the most popular band since…well, I can't think of another, and opportunity only knocks once, so they say. I'd be a fool not to make the most of it, don't you think? Perhaps we can arrange something the next time you're in England?"

Lucille swirled the champagne in her glass and took her time before replying. "Perhaps."

"Lonnie was your manager?" Dodo asked.

Lucille's lips hiked up on one side. "He was. After my daddy died, that is."

"Isn't it rather unusual that one of the musicians takes on that role?"

"My daddy and Lonnie had a manager long ago and he embezzled from them. It was an ugly business." Lucille laid heavy emphasis on 'ugly'. "Daddy was gutted. He vowed never to let anyone else manage his business. When he died, Lonnie honored that vow. Thankfully, he had learned a lot about the commercial side of things from my father," Lucille explained.

"So, Lonnie had a contact over here that he booked appearances with?" This could open up a whole new basket of suspects.

"He did. Man by the name of Neville Spoonbridge out of Manchester. We were supposed to meet with him on Wednesday, but I sent a telegram with our regrets."

If the band canceled, this Neville person would lose his commission, which would probably be a hefty sum. That ruled him out as a suspect in Dodo's mind. But the embezzler Lucille had mentioned was of interest.

"If you don't mind me asking, who was the man who defrauded your father? It could have a possible bearing on Lonnie's death."

A look of resignation settled on Lucille's face. "Man by the name of Basher. Lionel Basher. He pretended to be their friend but was running two sets of books and lining his own pockets. Neither Lonnie nor Daddy had much schooling, you understand. They put their trust in this man, and he took advantage. Daddy felt such a fool. After that, he paid someone to tutor him in mathematics and accounting."

"What happened to this Basher?"

"Went to jail." Lucille pushed shiny, black locks over her shoulder. "Far as I know, he's still there."

Or was he? This was worth following up on.

The food arrived and the talk became more casual. As usual, the French chefs had outdone themselves and every course was mouthwateringly delicious. Even the unassuming musicians were tucking in. But Dodo's mind was working nineteen to the dozen.

"Miranda, what's your story?" asked Cy as they tucked into the meat course with questionable manners.

Miranda repeated the story she had told Dodo the night of the murder.

"Our stories aren't so different," murmured Lucille. "Father-daughter team. Unknowns. It's a rags-to-riches tale."

"Not quite the riches yet, but we're getting there," agreed Miranda.

"Not if you keep spending the money before we make it," said Gerry in a playful tone.

"I'll thank you to keep your opinions to yourself," shot back Miranda with a laugh. "Don't you know you need to spend money to make money?"

"I don't think they meant go into the red," Gerry argued with good humor.

"How did you get into drumming?" Rupert asked him.

"School band, actually," he responded. "My school had some moth-eaten instruments in an old cupboard, and one of the teachers had the bright idea of starting an after-school band. My mam thought anything that kept me off the streets was a good idea and signed me up. The minute I

110

touched the drum I was hooked. The teacher let me take it home, and I practiced every minute I could, driving my family mad. But by the time I was fifteen, I was playing with a local band at weddings."

"And you, Fred? How did you come to play the piano so well?" Dodo asked the vacant-looking man who looked like a stray amongst the thoroughbreds at a Crufts dog show.

He shrugged. "Just born that way."

"What? You mean 'able to play'?" Dodo asked with disbelief. She herself had endured five torturous years of piano lessons and could barely play "Clair De Lune" with two fingers.

"Yeah. I just hear the tune in my head and then my fingers find the keys. It's like magic." His fingers opened in a chef's kiss.

"It's called 'playing by ear'," explained Miranda. "'Course to get that tone, it takes practice, but it's true. He only needs to hear a melody once and he can play it without sheet music, can't you Fred?"

Fred nodded with a toothy grin.

"Do you compose?" Dodo asked him.

"I—"

"I have to do that," Miranda interrupted. "And it's a labor of love, emphasis on the labor."

Dodo glanced at Fred who was now staring at his dinner plate.

"That takes true talent," commented Lucille. "We compose as a group. Trying out melodies and changing notes. Adding harmonies."

"How long does it take to write a new song?" Dodo asked the American woman.

"Depends," began Lucille. "Some songs almost write themselves and others take weeks. What about you, honey?"

"Same," replied Miranda. "Sometimes I'll wake up with a new melody playing in my head and I just have to write it down. Other times, I'm banging away on the piano for hours just to give my brain something to work with. The longest it ever took was two months. But it's the one I'm most proud of—'Baby Loves Me Right'."

"Oh! I really like that song," said Rupert. "It's in my personal collection. It's a great ballad."

"You really think so? Thank you!" gushed Miranda, melting all over the table.

They ordered dessert, and Dodo said, "If you'll excuse me, I need to powder my nose."

"I'll join you," said Miranda, pushing out from the table.

The bathroom at the Ritz was as opulent as the rest of the hotel. Dodo and Miranda entered their own stalls. By the time Dodo went to wash her hands, Miranda was already at the sink, repairing her lipstick.

"I suppose you're used to this kind of glamor," said Miranda, peering into the gilded mirror to check she had no lipstick on her teeth.

"Guilty," said Dodo. "I was lucky enough to be born into a life of luxury."

Miranda's mouth shrugged. "I don't hold it against you or anything. Not now I have it in my sights. I can almost taste the money, you know?"

Talk of money in the upper classes was frowned upon, but Dodo supposed that was because they didn't need to worry about where their next meal was coming from. She forgave Miranda the crass comment.

"I have no doubt you will be fantastically famous in no time. Your singing made my bones tingle," Dodo admitted.

"Really? It's so nice of you to say that." Miranda reached into the purse that was sitting open on the counter to get a powder compact. Dodo glanced down as the light caught something in the bag.

It was a pearl-handled gun.

Chapter 17

Dodo's jaw dropped as she met Miranda's confused stare. Then Miranda dropped her gaze, quickly flashing her troubled eyes up at Dodo. "It's not what you think."

"It's not a gun?"

"Well, yes, but it's for protection. My dad got it for me now that I travel a lot at night."

Dodo pushed out her bottom lip.

Miranda's face fell. "I didn't shoot Lonnie. How could I? I was singing on stage."

That much was true. But someone else could have used her gun to kill him, either by design or on impulse.

"Where was this gun the night of the murder?" Dodo demanded, pointing to the weapon.

"In my bag," replied Miranda, beads of sweat popping out on her upper lip in the brightness of the lights around the mirrors. "I swear."

"Who knew it was there?" Dodo persisted.

"Only the other mates in the band. It's not like I swing it around for fun. And my blokes were up on stage with me."

"But don't you see? Anyone could have taken it out of your bag while you were performing, killed Lonnie, and placed it back in the bag without you knowing." Which pointed the investigation directly at the members of Smokey Syncopation.

Miranda took in a sharp breath, looking to contradict Dodo, then blew the breath between her lips. "Cripes. You're right. Was it this kind of bullet that killed him?"

This was a great question. Having not been involved in any cases using guns to date, it was not a point Dodo had considered. "I don't know. I'll have to ask the inspector. Did you tell him you owned a gun?"

Miranda's head snapped back, fear leaking from every pore. "Not likely! He'd have arrested me on the spot."

Dodo could see why Miranda didn't trust the police, but it was unlikely the inspector would have done what she suggested since her alibi was iron clad. But she had no doubt he would have confiscated the weapon until it could be compared with the bullet that had killed Lonnie.

"I think you should hand it over to the police," suggested Dodo.

Miranda's arms jerked back across her chest. "I'll never get it back."

"I don't believe that's true, but perhaps I can call the inspector first and ask what caliber was used to kill Lonnie. If it's not the same, then I would say there was no need to disclose that you possess it."

Miranda's eyes scrunched tight before she whispered, "Alright. But if it *is* the same…"

"They will book the gun into evidence—"

"—and I'll never get it back." Her red lips pulled up in a pout.

"Let's cross that bridge when we get to it," said Dodo.

Now that the tension had abated, she noticed the bathroom attendant, engrossed in their heated conversation. Dodo tilted her head in the attendant's direction. "Let's go."

Miranda snapped the handbag's clasp.

"Everything alright? What took you?" whispered Rupert when Dodo slithered back into her chair.

"I'll tell you later," she said with a big, false smile at the rest of the table.

As they all said goodbye on the pavement outside the Ritz, Miranda and her musicians were the first to leave. Dodo figured Miranda was shaken by the events that had transpired in the bathroom, and the men looked in sore need of a pint.

114

Dodo realigned her thoughts. She hadn't yet addressed the questions with Lucille that she had concerning the telegram she had received from New Orleans. She and Rupert had devised a plan to address them in a more private setting. Putting all thoughts about the gun to the back of her mind for the time being, she nudged Rupert.

"Lucille. Gentlemen. Shall we have a nightcap at the bar?" asked Rupert.

"Don't mind if I do," said Dex with a mischievous grin.

"Me neither," agreed Cy, flattening his lips together, his fingers raised in a steeple, tapping each other with excitement.

Lucille's tired side eye indicated that she just wanted to go to bed, but Dodo needed answers.

"We won't keep you long," Dodo encouraged. "You put me on the case, and I have some things I need to discuss with you."

Lucille shrugged and they went back inside to the bar.

While the men went to order drinks, Dodo and Lucille found a table, and Dodo used the time alone with the singer to address the issues.

"Since you asked me to look into Lonnie's death, I have uncovered a few…things. Delicate things. Before running with them, I wanted to get your take. Newspapers are notoriously bad at getting their facts straight, I find."

Lucille's eyes widened. "Such as?"

Dodo glanced around to make sure no one could hear and leaned forward. "Is there a woman claiming to be Lonnie's daughter?"

Lucille threw back her head, and a deep, throaty laugh bubbled out.

"Honey, when you start making this type of money, *everyone* claims to be your daughter."

Dodo bristled. "So, you don't see this as a credible allegation?"

Lucille shook her finger. "Nuh-uh!"

115

"Alright, I'll cross that one off the list," said Dodo, retrieving her notebook and pencil. "How about the relationship between Lonnie and your father? Did they always get along?"

Lucille's eyes narrowed sharply. "You think my daddy came back from the dead and shot Lonnie?"

Lucille was running rings around her, leaving Dodo feeling a little embarrassed. "Let me rephrase that question," she said. "There was a newspaper article about a dispute over ownership of a certain club."

Bobbing her head, Lucille blinked. "The part about the dispute is true to a point, but the newspapers blew the whole thing way out of proportion. Daddy wanted to deed his share over to me, so he hired a lawyer and did the whole thing by the book. He asked Lonnie if he wanted to sell his share to me and mentioned a price. Lonnie thought the club was worth more than that. There was a disagreement, and daddy brought in someone to value the company. End of story. There was no falling out, and my father and Lonnie were the best of friends until Daddy's dying day."

"Are you the sole proprietor of the club now?"

"Nope. Unless Lonnie left his half to me in his will..." The start in her eyes indicated that she realized she had created a problem for herself. She put a hand to her lips. "I guess that's what the police might call a motive."

Dex and Cy sank into the luxury, leather club chairs. "Gotta get me one of these," said Cy with a wink. "What good is money if it can't buy you the finer things in life?"

"And how would a fine chair like that look in the hovel you call home?" asked Dex with a wink.

"Ain't no one gonna see it but me," said Cy, lifting one brow.

"You have a point there, brother," said Dex with a smile so broad it filled his whole friendly face.

With Lucille still reeling from the self-incrimination, Dodo directed her next question to the men.

116

"I hope this doesn't seem like prying," she began, "but I assume you all started with very little in the way of worldly goods and worked your way up. How has the money affected your life?"

Dex got very serious. "It means I don't never need to go hungry no more, little lady."

Dodo froze at his sincerity. "Was that a constant problem when you were young?"

He squeezed his face shut as if he were in pain, then relaxed. "Every single day." He pulled a large handkerchief from his pocket and wiped his eyes. "My mama had ten of us kids and my pops died when the youngest was seven. Mama had to go to work as a maid in a hotel, but it only covered the rent. Those of us who were old enough got work but they paid us so little we was always short of food." The large, angelic smile came back. "My mother is eighty-three, and my success has bought her a big 'ole home of her own with a fancy porch and a cupboard just a' burstin' with food."

Dodo had never had a hungry day in her life. "Have the rest of your siblings been as successful as you?"

His bottom lip came up to grab the top. "No, ma'am. Grace and Lincoln died 'afore they were eighteen, and the rest are good, honest folks who squeak by. I send them a little something each month to help make ends meet."

"Dex is a real saint," said Cy with no hint of sarcasm. "Me, I ain't got no family, and I bought myself a nice house off 'a Bourbon Street, whatever Dex might say about it. American dream right there. Own a piece of the land. I still have to pinch myself."

"There are no downsides to it?" asked Rupert, who had been listening intently. "The money, I mean."

Cy and Dex shared a look. "You mean the 'cousins' that come out of the woodwork like cockroaches for a loan," said Cy. "Sho' nuff! There are plenty of those."

117

"And what about the women who say they love you for your shining *personality*, but we all know it's really because of your healthy bank account," said Dex with a raspy chuckle. "It's hard to know who your real friends are, I reckon."

"Do people ever claim you stole their songs?" asked Dodo, thinking of the last question on her list.

A switch on the good mood in the room turned to 'off'.

Cy's shoulders stiffened and his mouth shrugged. "No. Why d' ya ask?"

"I thought I heard that someone accused the band of some such thing." Her voice trailed off and she searched their stoney faces.

"We got no reason to borrow trouble. Everything we produce is original. No matter what people might say," said Dex. His tone was final, and Dodo felt the heat.

Oh, dear!

"Do you like cricket?" asked Rupert, and Dodo wanted to kiss him.

"Never seen a match," said Cy, his rigid frame unwinding.

"Perhaps we can take you to one while you are here," Rupert suggested, and began explaining the finer points of cricket.

Lucille was still wound tight as a clam.

Chapter 18

Although it was early summer, the morning had been cold and wet. Dodo had asked Lizzie to look out a light cardigan to go over her summer frock.

"How was the matinée?" Dodo asked while her maid curled her hair.

As the tiny diamond on her left hand twinkled, Lizzie blushed. "It was so good. That Charles Lambert cuts a fine figure. I felt almost guilty sitting there holding Ernie's hand and finding the man on the screen so attractive."

Dodo smirked. "Isn't that the whole point of the silver screen? They want the actors to be so alluring that they become a guilty addiction and the public keeps handing over their hard-earned money to see the same film over and over again."

Lizzie gave a contented sigh. "Yes. Exactly."

"Rupert took *me* to see the house. It's chaos. Is Ernie really alright living in that atmosphere?"

Lizzie paused, the curling tong suspended over Dodo's head. "Do you know, I think he loves bossing those workmen around. He's never had authority over anyone before and he quite likes it." She chuckled. "Then when they all go home the silence is so welcome he doesn't feel lonely."

"Well, I'm glad to hear it. I couldn't live there."

Lizzie sucked in her cheek, and Dodo caught sight of the action in the mirror. "What's that look for?"

"But you might live there one day," said Lizzie with a coy hitch of her lip.

Dodo caught her gaze. "What do you mean?"

"Well, you know."

"Do I?"

"Don't you?"

Dodo flapped her arms. "Sometimes I do and sometimes I don't. Have you heard anything?"

With pursed lips, Lizzie looked down. "No. If Ernie knows anything he's keeping it quiet."

"I'm just impatient I suppose, and with Didi getting married before me…"

"I know exactly what you mean," agreed Lizzie. "But like you said, you wouldn't want to live there in all that pandemonium. He'll wait until it's all ready."

Dodo tapped her feet on the floor as if she were running. "Do you think so?"

"I know I don't have much experience, but it seems to me that men like to have everything in order before they ask a girl to marry them."

"Let's hope that's it and he doesn't have cold feet!"

"Inspector Crenshaw, how are you today?" He had sounded brassed off when he picked up her call.

"I am feeling some pressure to make an arrest in this Lonnie Chapman case, if you must know, and I don't quite have enough evidence yet."

"How frustrating for you, Inspector."

"Do you have anything for me?"

"Not yet, but I do have a question." She held her breath. In his current mood, he might just hang up on her.

"A question?" he growled.

"I was wondering if you knew what kind of gun Lonnie was shot with?"

She heard a lot of paper rustling. "They're still doing testing, but the preliminary results are that it was a larger pistol."

Not Miranda's little item then.

"Thank you."

"Why do you want to know?" he grunted.

"I have never investigated a crime where a gun has been the murder weapon and I am trying to expand my forensic knowledge. Is the strength of a gun determined by its measurement from end to end?"

She could almost feel the superior smile through the line. She had wagered that a little innocent declaration of ignorance would flatter the man. He gave her a short lesson on caliber.

"There, you see! You were just the man to help me." She was holding the piece of dirty cruise liner ticket in her hand. She hadn't resolved whether to disclose that she had found it or not before making the call, but given the inspector's current ill humor and considering that she did not even know if it was actually relevant, she decided to keep the matter quiet for the time being. "Well, thank you, Inspector. Now, I will let you get back to your job."

The offices of the *Princess Charlotte* travel agency were as regal as their namesake. Dodo had dressed with some attention to detail as if she were attending a royal garden party. When the officious clerk looked up and over his wire spectacles, she rewarded him with her most stunning smile and watched him visibly melt. She had rejected contacting them on the telephone for the very reason that she could not maximize the intensity of her presence to her advantage.

"How may I help you, miss?" The older clerk's voice had been rendered suitably wobbly, and the question was delivered through slack lips that had lost their battle with gravity.

"I really hope you can. Mother is extremely worried that something terrible has happened."

"Something terrible? Surely not." Pale eyes blinked behind strong lenses.

"Well, traveling all the way from America can be rather dangerous, and Mother is sure. She can feel it in her bones."

121

The clerk pulled up to his full height. "I can assure you that travel on our ship is one of the safest forms of transportation."

Dodo batted her lashes, and the poor man's defenses sunk a little farther.

"Is there something in particular that I can help with?" he asked.

"It's Anna. One of our parlor maids. She went to see her brother in America because he was in an accident. She was supposed to return on June the fifth, but she never arrived. It could be that she has delayed her passage and we never received the telegram, but it has us *so* worried." She brought her hands up in front of her chest. "Is there any way you could check the ship's manifest for me?"

His hooked nose quivered as his neck stretched out of the starched collar that held it bound. "Generally, we keep such things *confidential*." His chin dipped until it came in contact with his tie.

Dodo crumpled her face as if she were about to burst into tears all over his counter. His expression followed suit. "But I am sure I can make an exception since she is an employee of your illustrious family."

Dodo withdrew a lace hankie from her sleeve and wiped the imaginary tears away. "I can't tell you how grateful I would be."

"If you don't mind waiting?" He indicated the chairs behind Dodo.

He was gone not more than two minutes and returned holding a large leather-bound book to his chest.

"Miss?"

"*Lady* Emmeline Bonnington-Smythe," replied Dodo.

"Oh, I do apologize, my lady." He opened the ledger to the date in question and turned the book toward Dodo.

With a light laugh she ran a finger down the list of incoming passengers. Though tempted to stop on Lucille, Lonnie, Dex and Cy in first class, she ran down until she

122

found the steerage passengers, those who could only afford to travel in the bottom of the ship.

There were seventeen steerage passengers in total. Fourteen were clearly families, which left three passengers traveling alone. Two were men in their sixties, but one caught her attention. A Carl Mueller. Aged thirty-one. She glanced up and smiled at the clerk then ran a finger across the page to see if it listed his home address.

New Orleans, Louisiana.

"How are we to go about seeking this Mueller?" Rupert asked as they ate pickled winkles together on Westminster Bridge.

"It's a real needle in a haystack situation, isn't it?" she agreed. "I wish I could have asked to see the outgoing lists, but I thought that would be pushing my luck since I made up the story about a British maid returning from America."

"We don't even know what he looks like!" remarked Rupert.

The sharp flavor of the salty vinegar filled her mouth with pleasure as the conundrum filled her mind with frustration.

"David can't help me on this one. Is there anyone else we know that might be able to?"

An idea burned in Rupert's face. "What about Ronnie? He could poke about a bit in the underbelly of London life. I'll make it worth his while."

"Fabulous idea!" She gave him a vinegary kiss on the end of his nose. "Do you think, if this Mueller *is* an assassin, he would have stayed long after committing the deed?"

"Not likely, I'd say. Disappearing as soon as possible would be his safest bet. In and out before an investigation has even begun."

"So, what *do* we know about the fellow? We can tell Ronnie that he has an American accent, likely with the same lilting rhythm as Lucille and the band. That he is in his early thirties and may have carried a gun. It's not much to go on, but it's better than nothing. He can begin with the pubs on or near the Isle of Dogs." She slid another of the little, black seafood out of its shell with a needle. "Are we saying that it is one of the band that paid for the hit since this man came from Louisiana?"

"I think we are," said Rupert, a winkle suspended on his needle.

"I think I may have let my emotions cloud my deduction on this one. Lucille is such a charismatic figure, but I really cannot take what people tell me at face value without corroboration, even though she's the one who hired me. Lucille may be more eager to own the club outright than she is letting on. However, I don't know what the other two might have against him."

"You said there was a woman claiming to be his daughter," Rupert reminded her. "Not being recognized as kin could make a person really angry, especially if there's a lot of money at stake and they feel they have evidence to prove their case. That could prove to be a pretty strong motive."

"Lucille pooh-pooed the notion, telling me that it happened all the time because of the wealth they were accumulating, but you and the others were at the bar. There was no one to contradict her, and I took her words as gospel. Maybe another telegram is in order." She wiped her fishy fingers off with a napkin. "Then there's the plagiarism case. They all got pretty cagey about that. Makes me wonder if there is something to it, or at least that the person claiming it believes they have a case. A lawsuit of that kind could be worth thousands."

Ronnie had been more than happy for the work and within a couple of days asked Rupert and Dodo to meet him in Hyde Park.

"There was a man, answering the description you gave, at the Crown and Thistle in Limehouse the day before the murder. The publican remembers him because he was rude about the beer."

"Was he able to give a description?" asked Dodo, feeling her senses begin to tingle.

"He was short with dark hair and looked like his nose had been broken more than once."

Not the man calling himself 'Vlad'.

"Well done, Ronnie!" commended Rupert.

"There's more," said Ronnie. "He had a tattoo on his wrist. A skull and crossbones."

With the description of the American stranger in hand, Dodo and Rupert were back at the abandoned warehouse, hoping to find Willie. Rupert had brought the car, presuming it was the magic magnet that would lure the wily, young orphan out of his hiding place. The weather was overcast and threatening rain, sounds of the working docks all around them.

After kicking around for thirty minutes, Dodo declared. "I don't think we're going to find him today."

They opened the impressive car's doors and were just about to drop into the seats when a movement caught their eyes. Rupert winked and they stood, waiting.

"'Ello! Come to buy me more sweets?"

Willie was dressed in exactly the same clothes with a smudge of soot on his nose. His hair was sticking up in all directions, and as before, his toes were hanging out of large holes in the front of his boots.

"Would you like some?" Dodo asked.

Willie pulled a battered, grey bag out of his pocket. "I've still got some bull's eyes left. I let myself have one a day."

"Impressive restraint," said Rupert.

Willie looked confused. "That shows amazing self-control," explained Rupert. "Want to go for a ride?"

"'Cor, yeah!" And before they could invite him, Willie had installed himself in the little back seat.

"Where to?"

"Let's go down Port Street," said Willie. "I want me friends to see me."

"Right you are."

Before he started whooping and hollering, Dodo asked, "Willie, we're wondering if you saw a stranger here the day of the murder or the day before? A man with a strange accent, a crooked nose and a skull and crossbones tattoo on his wrist."

Willie pinched his lips. "Nope. I'd 'ave remembered a tattoo like that. News of it would 'ave passed round the Isle quick as lightening 'cos Old Mick used to have one on his arm just like it."

His words punctured her high expectations. *Drat!* Dodo was sure the shady man would have been lurking around the docks for at least a day before to scope out the landscape in preparation for the hit.

"How about you show us something we might not know about this place?" Rupert suggested to Willie. Dodo recognized it as an attempt to counteract her disappointment.

"'Ave you been to the tunnel?" asked Willie.

Dodo snapped her head around. "No! Where does it go?"

"Right under the river. All the locals know about it, but outsiders are always surprised. It takes you straight to Greenwich."

"Willie, you are full of revelations," said Dodo. "I'd love to see it."

Willie directed Rupert to the tunnel entrance, an ordinary red brick, glazed dome that would not have garnered a second look.

They stepped out of the car and Willie ran ahead. "There's a lift but I don't trust it. I always take the stairs."

Dodo and Rupert followed him down the narrow, circular steps that took pedestrians to the tunnel, deep under the river Thames. Dodo counted eighty-seven. Stark, electric lights reflected off plain, white tiles while Willie chattered like a happy parakeet, telling them of different escapades he had got up to in the tunnel.

The lively smile dropped, and his joyful expression transformed to fear. "I stay out of 'ere at night, though. Totally different type of customer at night." He clapped his hands. "I often go over in the late afternoon and dig through the bins of the restaurants. I forgot, but now that I'm down 'ere it reminds me. The day of the murder I was running late, and a gruff bloke bumped into me. 'E was a stranger. I could tell 'e wasn't from these parts. 'E sounded...odd."

Dodo's pulse leapt. "Did he sound American? Like the beautiful singer?"

Willie's dirty little face screwed into confusion. "What would that sound like?"

Dodo glanced at the ceiling before launching into a horribly amateurish rendition of a Southern accent that even made *her* cringe. She ignored Rupert, who was struggling not to laugh, and whacked him on the arm.

"Nope. Nothing like that," said Willie, with no hint of contempt.

The weighty burden of frustration tugged at her again. As they walked on, she began to consider her options. "How about like this?" she asked and tried to make her plummy tones sound as Scouse as she could manage.

Willie pointed his finger at her. "Yeah! That was it. Never 'eard anything like it."

On tenterhooks, Dodo asked, "Where did he go?"

"I followed 'im from a distance 'cause 'e didn't say sorry and 'e was carrying a pillow. I was worried 'e was

127

going to take my sleeping spot. But I made sure to keep to the shadows. Now that I think about it, 'e did go in the direction of your party, but it was way before it began."

Before Dodo knew it, they were climbing the stairs on the other side, emerging into one of her favorite spots in London, Greenwich, home of the Prime Meridian.

Trying to keep her rising hopes under control, another thought came to mind. "Willie, how did he smell?"

"Funny you should ask 'cos 'e stunk to 'igh heaven. Smokey. But not like a fire or nothin'. It was really strong and caught in my throat. Bloomin' awful, it was."

Chapter 19

Dodo stopped in her tracks.

Willie's shocking testimony turned everything she had thought about the case on its head.

At her request, he described the stranger to Dodo as she scribbled the details into her little notebook. Tall, stocky, red, curly hair, prominent, yellow teeth. But most importantly, Scouse.

Rupert kept glancing at Dodo as they walked farther into Greenwich, but she looked straight ahead, thinking. When they spotted an ice cream vendor with his cart, Rupert asked, "Would you like an ice cream, Willie?" Dodo was glad of the distraction as her intelligent mind fired with new possibilities about the murder.

The young child's eyes almost popped out of his head. "Are you kidding?"

A huddle of boys in school uniform surrounded the cart, and even as her mind was occupied, it struck Dodo that Willie did not attend a school. She thought back to what Fred had told her about life on the streets and wondered if Willie could even read.

Once they had each bought a cone, they ambled along, licking their ice creams while Dodo's brain continued to revise her theories. She had been looking at this all wrong. It wasn't one of his own band members that had killed Lonnie. It was someone in the *other* band, Crazy Train. What better alibi than being on stage at the time of the attack?

But why?

As Rupert and Willie blathered on about boats and ships, Dodo tried to remember all the things she had learned from her conversations with the British jazz band. There was Fred Garrett, the formerly homeless piano man who played by ear. Did he also have a knack for creating new music? The charge of plagiarism had certainly hit a nerve with the Americans. Dodo thought back to the conversation about composing at the restaurant. Had Fred said anything? No. It was Miranda that wrote their songs, she was sure. But Miranda was clearly in charge. What if Fred *did* compose? A man with a gift like his surely had ideas about original tunes. Could he have secretly sent a new piece of music to the famous band in New Orleans only to hear his very own melody in the next hit of Smokey Syncopation, earning the band thousands of dollars? It was entirely possible, though she wondered if he had the know-how to accomplish such a task. Then there was Gerry Waters. Did drummers compose? How proficient in the craft of music did one have to be to play the drums? Did he play another instrument? So many questions.

And then there was Miranda, a girl from a hard scrabble background who had proven to be indecently ambitious. A girl so progressive that she carried a gun in her handbag. It wasn't preposterous to think that such a woman had composed a song that she sent to New Orleans. She was certainly brazen enough. If she thought Smokey Syncopation had stolen her intellectual property, she was just the type of personality to orchestrate a malicious revenge. But she was impulsive and impetuous. Would she have the patience to undertake this type of slow, detailed and calculated retaliation?

As soon as Dodo got back to her mother's hidey hole, she made a call to the inspector. She hoped the police lab had now determined the exact caliber of the gun. She had promised Miranda that she would not tell the inspector that the singer carried a weapon, but that was before the bombshell that Willie had laid on them. Wasn't it probable that a woman who owned one gun had more stashed somewhere else?

"Hello, Inspector Crenshaw? This is Lady Dorothea. I have another question about the Lonnie Chapman murder."

A sound like a regurgitating bullfrog came down the line before he said, "Well, I'm not sure, depends on the question."

"I have information to share with you," she said to sweeten the pot.

She could almost hear his brain gauging the situation. "Alright. No promises though. What do you want to know?"

"Have you discovered the exact caliber of the gun that was used?" She crossed her fingers.

"It was a .45 standard military issue Webley Revolver."

"Aren't those rather loud?" she asked, remembering that the waiter thought he heard an echo from the champagne bottle.

"They are, but there was a lot of noise inside that could have drowned it out. Or there is the possibility that the killer used something to silence the noise."

Here was an idea that had not occurred to her.

"So, what have you got for me?" he asked.

"Miranda has a gun, a .25. But it may mean she has others."

Through a smirky chuckle he replied, "Old news. I've seen the gun you are referring to and it is the caliber you have described. Not the caliber used to kill Mr. Chapman. My men have recently searched her room and bags and that of the other band members and found no more weapons."

Miranda would think his search had originated with Dodo informing the inspector about what she had seen in the bathroom. She would view it as a betrayal.

"How did she react at the intrusion?" asked Dodo.

"She was fuming, but she did not resist and swore up and down it was the only gun she had."

"Did you confiscate it?" Dodo asked.

"No, since it's not illegal and it was not the murder weapon."

"Is Miranda Masters no longer a suspect?"

"I did not say that. She is still a person of interest." He paused. "If that is all, I have work to do."

His snide attitude had awakened the fighter in her and she did not want him to think she had nothing else to offer. She had a reputation to uphold, after all.

"Are you aware that Mr. Chapman was part owner of a club in New Orleans?" She was sure he did, but she didn't want to show all her cards from the start.

"That all you've got? I knew that the day after the murder."

The chauvinism in the inspector's tone was almost more than she could bear. She was definitely *not* going to mention her discovery about Willie and the Rude Liverpudlian, as she now thought of him. He didn't deserve it. And she needed to follow up on it anyway.

"Are you also aware that Miss Bassett is the other owner?" she continued.

"Another swing and a miss," replied the inspector using cricket terminology.

His tone made her mad, but if she did not give him something valuable, she would lose credibility and be unable to pump him for more information in the future.

"Miss Bassett claims not to know the contents of Lonnie's will, but she realizes that we only have her word on that, and if Lonnie has left her his half of the club, this gives her a motive."

"That very well could be," replied the inspector. "We have been in contact with the police in New Orleans and they have confirmed that Mr. Chapman had no other family. Which brings up another problem. The will. Generally, the will is read after the funeral. But the difficulties in transporting the body back to America have been explained to Miss Bassett, and she has decided to have the body cremated here in a small, private ceremony and to take the ashes back to Louisiana."

A pit opened in Dodo's stomach. She had no idea of any of this. "But the investigation is ongoing," murmured Dodo.

"Indeed. I informed Miss Bassett that the contents of the will *must* be read before they return, so the cremation has been arranged for—well, you probably know."

Was he baiting her?

"Of course. Miss Bassett and I were discussing it just today," she lied.

"Well, if that's all you have for me...?"

Dodo was furious. She was being dismissed. But she felt that the policeman had well and truly trumped her and that she had been unable to give him anything worthy of maintaining her credibility. But she was adamant that she was not going to tell him about the stranger. Mind racing, she searched for some tantalizing tidbit that would send him on a fool's errand.

Bingo!

"What about the American with a tattoo who was seen in Limehouse the day before the murder? The one who came over on the *Princess Charlotte* the same day as the band?"

The silence indicated that this time she had hit her target. And even though Willie's story now led her to believe that the American had nothing to do with the murder, she felt no guilt at laying the false clue at the arrogant inspector's feet. After all, a clue was a clue.

"Tattoo? Have you found him? Do you have a name?"

"Not yet, though I have people on the problem. But the tattoo is a skull and crossbones on the wrist. The owner of the Crown and Thistle in Limehouse made a positive identification."

"Is the individual still in the country?"

133

"That I don't know, but I am sure with your resources you can find out from the shipping office of the *Princess Charlotte*, Inspector."

An indecent amount of grumbling indicated that Inspector Crenshaw was writing things down. "And when were you going to tell me about this foreigner?"

"Am I not telling you now, Inspector? And I happen to know he is from New Orleans."

"May I ask how you came by this knowledge?"

"I can't give away all my secrets. I'm sure you understand."

There was more mumbling before he said, "I'll send some uniforms to Limehouse. See if we can't smoke him out. Thank you, Lady Dorothea."

"Think nothing of it, Inspector."

She tried to squeeze out some guilt for her actions, but the inspector's misogynist tone had muddied the moral waters, and she hung up feeling rather smug.

Picking up the phone again, Dodo called the hotel and asked for Lucille.

"How are you feeling today?"

"Awful! Each day that passes knocks in another nail of reality. Lonnie is not coming back."

"Do you need any help with a funeral, or, you know, to navigate the British customs?" Dodo crossed her fingers.

"Oh, that's very kind of you, Dodo, but I've decided to have a private cremation here and organize a huge memorial in New Orleans after I return. Everyone in town will want to honor the man. Wanna come?"

The invitation caught Dodo off guard. "I-I w-well—"

A syrupy laugh erupted from Lucille. "Well, well, well. The great English Lady is lost for words. I bet that doesn't happen very often!"

Dodo had traveled extensively in Europe but had never set foot in America. As she let the idea marinate, the invitation began to increase its appeal.

"You just caught me off guard, Lulu. You hardly know me. Are you sure?"

"I feel like I do know you, sugar. Whaddya say?"

"My sister is getting married in July—"

Lucille interrupted her. "A celebration this big will take at least four months to organize. That enough time, honey?"

"In that case, count me in!" declared Dodo, making a prompt decision.

Lucille did not bring up the will and Dodo did not find a suitable opening. She would make sure to see her before the band left the country and try again. That is, if she hadn't already caught the murderer. Since they only had Willie's testimony about the Rude Liverpudlian and had not found him or anything to corroborate his existence, she decided not to tell Lucille and get her hopes up in case it proved to be another dead end.

Dodo had one more phone call to make. Since it had been several days since the murder, and Dodo's sights were now set on Miranda and crew, she called David to see if there was any scuttlebutt around town about Crazy Train.

"Have you recovered?" she asked him.

"Do you know, I've come to the realization that I am not the courageous man I thought I was. I keep having nightmares about...it." The usual cocky, devil-may-care attitude was absent.

"Poor David," she crooned. "What are you doing to soothe yourself?"

"I've taken a few days off work and laid it on thick with several of my lady friends who have come round to nurse the ailing patient and bring food and wine."

"Sounds perfect."

"Of course, my first choice of nurse is busy trying to catch the murderer."

Dodo ignored the barb. "So?"

"I may have heard that they had to move hotels."

"Yes, because they did not expect to stay this long in the city."

Instead of being upset that Dodo already knew this piece of gossip, David added, "That may well be part of it, but that's not the whole truth, darling. There were claims that they were hosting a fourth, *unregistered* guest and had inflicted some damage to the room. When confronted, though, Miss Masters denied the accusation vehemently, making a big scene and declaring that they had never been treated so badly and that they would take their business elsewhere."

Dodo gripped the phone.

The tattooed man?

Chapter 20

The Partridge was a proper, respectable hotel near Tower Hamlets. Dodo had decided to represent herself as a reporter for *Ladies Journal Magazine*. Avoiding the front desk, she ran up the front stairs in search of a chamber maid. She didn't have to search for long. A young girl in her late adolescence was pushing an overburdened cart, towering with towels and sheets.

"Excuse me," Dodo began. "I'm wondering if you might be able to help me?"

The girl looked up, caution behind her eyes. "What do you mean?"

"I'm from *Ladies Journal* and I heard that the jazz band *Crazy Train* were staying here a few days ago." As she spoke, she withdrew a silver coin from her purse. The maid's eyes fixated on the money in Dodo's hand. "Our readers are very interested in Miss Miranda Masters, and I was hoping to get some inside scoop."

The girl looked back along the corridor then beyond Dodo. "I was their maid," she whispered, eyes back on the silver coin.

Eureka!

"How fortunate," said Dodo. "I'm wondering if Miss Masters has any preferences with food or her room, you know, things like that? What is your name?" Panic manifested in the young girl's features and Dodo backtracked. "I don't need to put it in my piece of course. Don't you worry."

Discreetly, Dodo offered the coin to the maid, and her tense shoulders dropped. "It's Betty, miss."

Dodo extracted another coin but kept it between her gloved fingers. Betty relaxed. "Miss Masters likes breakfast in bed. Is that the kind of thing you want to know?"

"Exactly," replied Dodo in a sugary voice.

Betty dropped her own even lower. "That lovely red hair? It's a—"

The guest next door came out of their room and Betty dipped her head while Dodo pretended to use an invisible key to enter the door they were standing next to. As soon as the guest was out of earshot, Betty resumed. "It's a wig."

Dodo pretended to be astounded. "You don't say!"

She pulled out her notebook and acted as if she were writing everything down, which the coin made difficult. She folded it into her palm and slipped it to the maid who couldn't help licking her lips.

"What color is her real hair?"

Betty's face came alive. "Same as mine!"

"Well! That is a surprise!" She scratched away with the pencil. "Any inclination for unusual foods?" Dodo continued.

Betty went on to list all the things Miranda had requested while Dodo made the expected exclamations.

"Did she treat you well?" asked Dodo.

"Oh yeah! I told my mum that I like the band even more now that I've met them. All of them were very kind— though I did have trouble understanding them sometimes." She giggled. "That's why I didn't want to tell on them just now. They were so nice."

Dodo raised her brows, pencil at the ready.

Betty checked the corridor again. "I wasn't supposed to see, but I was cleaning a room down the hall, and I saw a stranger come out of Mr. Water's room. It was pretty early, but I didn't think much of it. But then, when I went to clean the room later, it was obvious that someone had slept on the settee in the room. That's totally against hotel policy. I *had* to tell Mr. Pritchett."

Dodo assumed him to be the hotel manager.

"What did he do?"

"He came with me to the room, as I hadn't cleaned it yet. There was a small bed pillow on the settee and a blanket from the wardrobe. Then he picked up the pillow to take it into the bedroom and gasped. I turned to see what was up and there was a ruddy great hole in the middle."

Betty slipped the money in the pocket on the front of her apron. "Mr. Pritchett got all red and left the room muttering. I heard from Pete the porter that when the group returned later, Mr. Pritchett confronted them, right there in the lobby. Miss Masters got all hoity toity and said she didn't know what he was talking about and how dare he accuse them of such conduct and didn't he know who they were? Mr. Pritchett said she could be the king of England, but if they hosted unpaid guests and destroyed hotel property, he would ask them to leave.

"Apparently, Miss Masters tossed her head and declared that she wouldn't spend another night in an establishment that made a habit of falsely accusing its important clients of misbehaving. They left right away."

Holding her breath, Dodo asked, "Could you describe the man you saw?"

Betty narrowed her eyes. "Why would your readers want to know that?"

Dodo did her best to look sheepish. "They wouldn't. But can you blame a girl for enjoying a bit of gossip?"

"You won't put this in the article, right? Miss Masters was lovely to me and I wouldn't want this to be made public."

Dodo drew an invisible cross over her heart. "You have my word, Betty."

"I didn't get a good look at him because I was so far away, but he was tall, with red, curly hair and a funny-shaped nose."

The elevator started to whir, and Betty glanced at her watch. "I need to get back to work."

"Of course." Dodo searched in her bag and pulled out another coin.

"Thank you, miss," said Betty before disappearing into the room.

🎷

"So, do you believe Miranda?" asked Rupert as they drank fresh lemonade outside a bistro in Leicester square.

"That she didn't know about the extra guest?" Dodo crinkled her nose. "I want to. I really like her rags-to-riches story—well, almost to riches."

"Let's say she *did* know and the performance in the hotel lobby was to save face."

"That means the assassin was working for the whole band and it would be all over for Crazy Train before it really started."

"And if she really didn't know?"

"Then we may have found our murderer. Gerry. But what is his motive? Lonnie had not been to England before, and Gerry has never left the country, as far as I know."

Rupert emptied his glass. "What are you going to do now?"

"I suppose I need to confront Gerry," she responded.

"That seems unnecessarily dangerous," said Rupert with alarm. "Can't you send an anonymous letter or something?"

Dodo had unwittingly placed herself in dangerous situations before. She had no intention of doing so on purpose. "Good idea. Much safer. Perhaps we can say that we have a witness from the party who saw something, and that Gerry should come clean to the police, or we'll send a tip to the papers."

Chapter 21

After she dispatched a telegram to Gerry, something Betty had said was tickling at the back of Dodo's active brain, but she couldn't quite put her finger on it. She thought perhaps talking to Willie again and getting a more detailed description of the 'Rude Liverpudlian' would jog her memory. And besides, she wanted to treat the little ragamuffin to something again. He had woven himself into her heart.

Pulling up in the roadster in the yard of the derelict warehouse, she looked around for the telltale rustling but heard nothing.

"Let's get out and see if he's in the building," she suggested.

The crisp sound of her shoes echoed, and a couple of pigeons fluttered across the ceiling.

"Willie!" She walked to the Green Room and, opening the door, called again. "Willie!" A dark shadow on the floor in the darkness made her heart jump into her throat.

"Rupert, get your torch, please."

When he returned, she showed him where to shine the beam. Her pulse dropped to normal as the light showed a moth-eaten blanket and another rolled into a sort of makeshift pillow. Evidence that Willie had been there.

"Perhaps if we just wait. He'll return to his lair in time," said Rupert with a grin.

"Then let's wait outside." It was an overcast day and little of the dim daylight penetrated the warehouse. It felt cold and damp and just a little spooky.

Dodo found a short wall to sit on and they looked out, past the buildings on the other side of the yard to the sliver of river. "What about treating him to ride on the ferry?" In spite of there being a foot tunnel, the ferry still operated, but as far as she could tell, it did not go very often.

"Maybe he doesn't like the water," said Rupert. "Children who live by the river see its dark side. I would imagine he has a great respect for it."

Dodo shrugged. "Let's ask him."

They watched sparrows scratch around for food that was not there and the odd mouse scurry across the ground. Still no Willie.

"Let's take a turn and see if he's playing in the streets," suggested Rupert.

Cruising along, they swerved to avoid games of football and hopscotch, keeping their eyes peeled for the little urchin. A renewed sense of unease began to crawl its way under Dodo's skin.

"Stop the car," she demanded, seeing the same group of little amateur football players for the third time.

"I say!" she called. The boys stopped playing and the one nearest to them ran a sleeve under his runny nose. "Have you seen a boy called Willie?" she asked.

The boys shook their heads, and after admiring the shiny vehicle, returned to their game. "Let's keep trying," said Dodo. "I can't explain it, but I have an ominous feeling."

They stopped at every group of children to ask but no one had seen the dirty imp. One older boy approached Dodo. "My mum don't let me play with 'im," he explained. "And neither do the other mums. They think he's a bad example because he don't 'ave no parents or an 'ome. Mum's worried I'll get nits or something. But there are a group of street kids that hang out by the bank at low tide. You could try there." He pointed in the direction they should go.

"Thank you!" said Dodo as Rupert pulled away.

They soon found the group of Fagin-worthy children, playing in the mud by the river as the tide was out. This produced a conundrum, as Dodo was wearing new, buck leather shoes. Rupert pulled as close to the river wall as possible and began to shout.

"Hello! I was wondering if any of you could help me." After a brief stare, the children went back to digging in the mud. Rupert slid his hand into a pocket and pulled out a thruppenny bit, holding it high. "I'll make it worth your while," he cried, holding the coin aloft between his thumb and index finger.

The four boys began to scramble out of the mud and up the bank, mouths open.

"Whaddya need, guv?" asked a boy with ginger hair that needed a good brush.

"We're looking for Willie," Dodo explained. "We need to talk to him. It's rather important."

"Ain't seen 'im today, but that's not unusual. 'E sometimes disappears for days and then shows up like a new penny." The boys' eyes had not left the coin.

"'E was 'ere yesterday," said another boy missing his two front teeth, clearly hoping that this information was deemed sufficient for the thruppence.

"Do you know where he sleeps?" asked Dodo, remembering the blankets on the Green Room floor.

"Never stays in one place too long 'case the workhouse ladies find us—'im," said the older boy.

Dodo had a vivid vision of a life lived on the edge with no one to have their backs or provide love and comfort, and she felt a stinging knot form at the back of her throat.

Rupert fished in his pocket again and found three more coins, two pennies and a farthing. He gave them to the boys, whose eager, shining eyes made Dodo's own prickle.

"Thanks boys!" Rupert saluted as he pulled away.

"I think we are out of luck," said Rupert. "Maybe we should try tomorrow."

Dodo could not ignore the sense of urgency in her chest. "Let's go back and wait a little longer."

Rupert rubbed his thumb over her knuckles. "If you like."

On their return, the building was as deserted as when they had left. "Let's give it ten minutes," she begged.

"I'm in no hurry," he said as they returned to wait in the car.

Time ticked by slowly, and it was evident that Willie was not going to come back any time soon.

"Thanks for humoring me," she said with a sad smile.

Rupert put the car in gear and depressed the clutch.

BANG!

Chapter 22

Dodo's eyes nearly shot out of her head.

Hand to her mouth, she turned toward the back of the car coming face to face with another street boy whose face was covered in smut.

Relief washed over her. "You scared us to death!"

"Sorry, missus," said the boy. "But I only just got back and 'eard you was lookin' for Willie." His expression dripped with fear.

She held out a hand. "You know where he his?"

The urchin's face dropped. "'E's got 'im!"

The knot returned to Dodo's stomach. "Who is 'he'?"

"I dunno, but 'e talks like a foreigner and 'e smells funny."

Dodo and Rupert locked eyes.

She took a deep breath. "What is your name?"

"Mikey. Look, I followed 'em for ages, but then I thought I should go for 'elp."

"Can you start at the beginning?" she asked.

Mikey started dancing from foot to foot. "It might be too late!"

"Jump in and show us where to go," demanded Rupert.

Mikey scrambled up the back of the car and into the jump seat. The level of his concern for Willie was so high it was as if he didn't even notice the magnificent car.

"That way!" he pointed, urgency in every word.

They traveled along the busy street filled with dock workers until Mikey cried, "Now that way." Rupert glanced over his shoulder to see which way the boy was pointing. Toward the river.

"That way!"

Dodo recognized this as the route they had taken to the tunnel to Greenwich. Panic stood in the wings, but she commanded him to depart, forthwith.

"Now straight on."

The isolated, red brick entrance to the tunnel was in sight. Rupert pulled to a stop behind another building and the little boy jumped out. "Come on!" His whisper was low and urgent as he ran, bent over. Dodo and Rupert followed.

Mikey did not head for the tunnel but for a ramshackle hut some fifty feet away. He turned, putting a stubby finger to his lips. They crouched behind a bush.

"You know what happens to little boys what nark?" came the thick cadence of a Liverpudlian accent.

Dodo's face puckered. Did the fiend have Willie?

"They are never 'eard of again!" came the deep voice.

A whimper floated through the gaps in the walls of the hut and wrapped around Dodo's heartstrings. "Rupert, we must do something!"

"First rule of combat; don't go into an unknown situation if the suspect may be armed."

Dodo twisted on her haunches to Mikey. "Did you see a gun?"

His head moved once. "No. That bloke don't need no gun. He's big as a monster."

Think, think!

The story of the Israelites and the walls of Jericho came to mind, and she sent up a prayer of thanks.

"We have to make the awful demon think there are a lot of us out here, and we have to pretend we are the police."

Rupert's eyes shone with questioning. "And how are the three of us supposed to do that?"

"Mikey, we met some boys digging in the mud further downriver. Do you know them?"

"Yeah. Some of 'em is me mates."

"Run like the wind and fetch them. Tell the boys there will be a reward. Quick!"

146

Mikey turned on his heels as the invisible ogre hollered, "Who did you tell?" The sound of a smack and a small yelp made Dodo's stomach roll.

"No one! I swear!" The habitually overconfident Willie now sounded small and frightened.

"That's not what I hear," cried the menacing voice.

"I didn't, guvnor. I promise! Just let me go. I'll never tell a soul." The words shattered into tears. It was all Dodo could do to stay put.

"The only men who don't tell tales are the dead ones."

Dodo gasped.

"I knew the day I saw you staring at me in that blessed tunnel you'd come back to haunt me. Should have killed you that night before I killed the American. I'm getting sentimental in my old age—and it's come back to bite me!"

"No!" cried out Willie. "No, please don't! I'll disappear and never tell a soul."

"Keep your voice down or I'll clip you again." They could hear the sound of footsteps pacing. "Got any family?"

"Yeah, my mum will wonder where I am if I'm not back for tea soon. My uncle's a copper."

Clever boy! Give him reasons to be careful.

"Why should I believe you?"

"'Cause it's true, guv." The wet little voice was breaking her heart.

A shuffling sound caught her attention, and the four boys came creeping to them behind the bush.

"What's the plan?" asked Rupert.

"Yours is the only voice deep enough to make an impact," she said to him. Then addressing the boys, she said, "I need you to make murmuring noises as deep as you can. We will stand in a ring around the shack and make a heck of a noise while Rupert shouts out loud. Can you do that?"

147

"Anything to save Willie," said the older boy from the beach.

"Let's all grab rocks and knock them together. We want to make as much noise as possible—but as if we are a crowd of policemen. Understand?"

Five solemn faces nodded, and they stooped to pick up rocks.

Positioning the boys around the hut with Rupert near the door, Dodo gave a hand signal. She and the boys made low murmuring sounds around the wooden shack and Rupert raised his voice, making it as deep as possible.

"Police! Police! Come out with your hands up! We have you surrounded!"

The hut went silent as Dodo and the boys kept murmuring and knocking the rocks together.

No one emerged.

Rupert tried again. "We are here to arrest you for the murder of Lonnie Chapman. There is nowhere to run. There are thirty of us, and some are armed."

The door to the hut creaked open a crack and Dodo waved her arms for the boys to get louder. If they could confuse the suspect enough, they would have the upper hand.

"We will give you to the count of ten!" cried Rupert. "One, two, three—"

The door to the hut shot open, with the suspect holding a beefy arm around Willie's skinny neck. The man's eyes flashed back and forth. Assessing the danger and seeing Rupert, he let out an evil bark of laughter.

Behind him, Dodo raised her arm, and with a jump, smashed the rock against the side of the kidnapper's head. He crumpled to the ground like a paper doll.

From Joshua and the Canaanites to David and Goliath.

Willie sprinted away from his giant captor straight into Dodo's arms. She wrapped him in a bear hug, her mouth against the top of his filthy little head.

148

All the other boys were cheering and hooting.

"I'll get some rope from my car," said Rupert, his cheeks flushed. "Don't know how long the brute will be out. Best to tie him up long before he regains consciousness."

♪

The ornery police inspector was fighting against a smile. "You managed to best this monster?"

Dodo bit her lip. "I had help, Inspector."

As soon as they had secured the murderer, Rupert had driven off in search of a telephone to contact Scotland Yard. It had taken them exactly half an hour to get to the hut during which time the hulking beast had come to, breathing out threats against his jailers while the boys danced around, taunting him. Willie had not left Dodo's side.

"Why do I have the feeling you sent me off in the wrong direction?" Crenshaw said, pushing his hat back from his face with a finger.

Dodo assumed a look of angelic innocence. "Was there no stranger from New Orleans who traveled steerage the same day as the jazz band? And did he not have a noticeable tattoo and appear around the location of the murder?"

The inspector's mustache danced a jig. "There was, but I cannot shake the impression that you knew he was not the murderer."

"How could I, a mere amateur, know that he wasn't the killer? He certainly hit many of the checklist items to indicate that he was the culprit. Wouldn't you agree, Inspector?"

"Humph!"

"Anyway, you're here now and can collar the real malefactor in a blaze of glory." She beamed at him from beside Willie.

"I shall want a full statement from both of you." He pointed a finger at her.

"I shall be more than happy to cooperate, Inspector."

"Sir!" called a constable, who was one of a trio wrestling with the killer to get him into the police car.

The inspector tipped his hat and walked away tsking.

"I don't like him," said Willie, rubbing his eyes.

"He's alright," contradicted Dodo. "Once you get past that grumpy crust."

"Can we get another ice cream?" he begged in a tiny voice.

Dodo had yet to hear how he had come to be in the 'Rude Liverpudlian's' clutches. "I'm sure if we explain to the inspector that you will be back and ready to answer his questions, he won't object."

"Will—will you stay with me while he questions me?"

"Of course."

After checking with the police, they drove Willie to the ice cream cart. Once he had licked half of it, she asked, "So, what happened?"

"I was minding me own business when one of the other boys says there's a scary giant asking for me. I told 'im to describe the bloke but I knew who it was, even before 'e did. Then I hid.

"But a mouse wandered into my 'iding spot and I couldn't resist and picked 'im up. I must 'ave made a noise, 'cause the next thing I know, 'e's 'auling me up by the scruff of my neck and dragging me to that shack." A sob escaped, and he looked to see if she had noticed. Dodo pretended she had not. "I thought I was a goner."

While she gently squeezed his arm, Willie licked the ice cream furiously. When it was all gone, he said, "I'll owe you forever."

"No need. You helped us solve the case, Willie. Miss Bassett will be so grateful. We couldn't have done it without you. So, we're even."

"Well, anytime you're on the Isle of Dogs, I 'ope you'll come and see me."

She swallowed. "You can count on it."

Chapter 23

Willie was a loner.

The other boys who had helped in the capture of the 'Rude Liverpudlian', who was known by the unlikely name of Banger, were filling Dodo and Rupert in on life on the streets on the Isle of Dogs. Unlike the gang in Dicken's *Oliver*, this little troop did not have an adult authority figure who made them steal. In fact, the only things these boys stole were from dustbins. Things people no longer wanted.

Each of them was an orphan who had been treated so badly in orphanages that they had escaped and come to the dock area. They formed a loose coalition, shunned by the local inhabitants, who looked out for each other. Some of them had formed close ties and friendships, but Willie kept them all at arm's length. It hurt less when people left if you didn't get too close; either for the great beyond, or just to move on.

But the near-death experience had made Willie crave human company—at least for the time being. His scallywag companions pumped his arms and slapped him on the back as he told his side of the story, and they told him theirs.

Dodo thought Willie might stay within the circle of their protection for a week or more. She hoped so. Then he would be sure to go back to his deserted buildings. Alone.

None of the boys could read and none of them could see the need. As soon as they were fourteen, they all had plans to join the navy. Even Willie. A boy named Bob had signed on two years before and had come back a few months ago to tell them about his adventures and all the money he had earned. And at least the Great War was over, and they wouldn't have to fight.

After the inspector had questioned Willie, she and Rupert settled him back with his friends. She bid him a tearful goodbye with a tender heart.

When she had recovered her composure, they traveled to Scotland Yard to give their statements.

Before leaving, they stopped by the inspector's office. He was groaning while pressing an ice bag to his face. When he removed it, they saw the enormous black-and-blue shiner beneath. Apparently, Banger had not been a fan of imprisonment.

However, while Dodo and Rupert had been giving their own statement of events, Banger had been singing like the proverbial bird. His real name was Frank Waters, brother to Fred.

Fred! Dodo had got it wrong!

"It was an honest mistake," said the inspector with unexpectedly good grace. "Frank had been dossing down in Gerry's hotel room because it had a settee, unlike his brother's. The maid steered you in the wrong direction because she saw Banger come out of Gerry's room, not Fred's, and then seen that he had slept there.

"According to Banger's own testimony, Gerry had no idea he was in London to kill Lonnie Chapman. The brothers told him that Fred thought it would be a bit of a lark to see London, since he could stay with his brother for free in a swanky hotel.

"They had all kept Banger's presence a secret from Miranda, who disapproved of Fred's violent older brother."

"How ironic," said Dodo. "Both Fred and his brother had been street children too. You'd think he would have had some compassion for poor Willie."

"I think he did," contradicted the inspector. "But for that, he would have killed Willie from the minute he saw the little chap watching him."

Dodo felt a chill run through her.

153

"But then Banger heard rumors that might implicate him and suspected that Willie had become a liability, a loose end, and Banger had to get rid of him to save his own neck."

"What was the motive?" asked Rupert.

"Was it because Fred thought Lonnie had stolen his song?" Dodo asked.

Inspector Crenshaw's eyes popped. "Now, how did you know that?"

"Lucky guess," she admitted. "One of the scandals surrounding Lonnie in New Orleans was the accusation of plagiarism. When I brought up the other news stories, the band members swept the rumors away, but that one seemed to irk them all, so I figured there might be something to it. And if Fred was gifted in playing the piano, why not in composing too?"

"I owe you an apology, Lady Dorothea," confessed the inspector, stroking his mustache. "I underestimated you."

"Never underestimate Dodo," warned Rupert with a chuckle. "She never ceases to amaze me."

The inspector replaced the ice bag back over his injured eye. "You hit the nail on the head, m'lady. It seems that Fred was not only a natural pianist; he could compose too, as you guessed. According to Banger, tunes would come to him all the time. But Miranda made it clear from the beginning that she was in charge of composition and wouldn't even listen to his suggestions. And since she and her father had rescued him from starving on the streets, he didn't push it.

"But once he had learned to read, not only words but also music, he was able to write his creations down. One day, he heard a record by Smokey Syncopation on a gramophone and felt a kinship with the style. He found out the name of the band and sent some music to Lonnie in Louisiana asking his advice.

154

"He heard nothing. But Crazy Train was starting to gain recognition and he forgot about it. Until a year later, when Smokey Syncopation had a wild hit. It was Fred's song. Or so he believed."

A secretary knocked and came in with a painkiller and a glass of water on a tray. "Thank you, Gwen," said the inspector. "Just what I need." Gwen nodded to Rupert and Dodo and left without a word. The inspector picked up the white pill and washed it down with the water.

"Now, where was I?"

"Fred believed Lonnie had stolen his song and made a lot of money," Dodo reminded him.

"Oh, yes. Fred wrote and wrote to Lonnie, asking for his fair share of the royalties and credit for the melody but received no answer. Lonnie was rich. Fred had grown up with nothing. Eking out a life on the streets had hardened Banger, and he stirred Fred up, convincing his brother the money was rightfully his, that he deserved it."

"When we asked Dex what he was most grateful for from his fame, he said it was knowing he would never be hungry again," said Dodo. "It was probably a driving force for the two brothers."

"I can't imagine, thankfully," responded the inspector. "But I don't wonder. Anyway, when Miranda mentioned she had heard through the grapevine that the organizer of a secret party in London was looking for a backup band for Smokey Syncopation, Fred and his brother came up with their dastardly plan. What better alibi than being on stage at the time of the murder?"

"That was the very thing that was a sticking point for me," said Dodo.

The inspector leaned back in the chair, hands behind his head. "Banger was supposed to get in and out of the Isle like a ghost, coming over through the tunnel then disappearing the same way. But that child had seen him. As I said, I reckon he didn't kill Willie right away because he saw himself in the lad. But in the end, his hesitation to get rid of him ruined everything. The police were asking questions, and Gerry had received an anonymous telegram about the guest in his room and threatening to go to the police, which he did not understand at all and mentioned it to Fred."

"That was from me, thinking the murderer was Gerry and trying to poke the bear," admitted Dodo feeling horrible. "It seems like it backfired and endangered Willie."

"Unfortunately, yes. It was time to get rid of the witness—the boy."

"Poor, poor Willie." She looked up. "But why on earth was a lad from Liverpool smoking French cigarettes?"

"He found a full packet at the dock in Merseyside when he was younger and got a taste for them. It was his guilty pleasure."

"And became his downfall," she commented.

"Will they both be prosecuted for the murder?" asked Rupert.

"We will certainly push for it," said the inspector.

"I suppose the gun was a holdover from the war?" Dodo remarked.

"Though in theory, soldiers were supposed to surrender their uniforms and weapons, some kept such items as souvenirs," agreed the inspector.

Dodo slapped Crenshaw's desk, making him and Rupert start. "The pillow! That's what has been at the edges of my mind. Banger used it as a silencer, didn't he?"

"Right again, m'lady."

"When Willie first mentioned the pillow, I assumed it was for sleeping. Even when the maid said there was a hole in one of the feather pillows at the hotel, it didn't sink in," Dodo added. "But I see it now. One of the feathers had actually stuck to the bottom of Rupert's shoe that night. The evidence was there all along."

"Like so often, the answer is in the small details," said the inspector, shaking his head.

Dodo and Rupert stood, and the inspector scrambled to his feet, extending his hand like an olive branch, the other holding the ice pack to his face.

"Though I did not do myself any favors, it has been a pleasure working with you, Lady Dorothea. Your reputation is well earned."

"Thank you, inspector."

As they reached his door, an image of the sepia picture in Lonnie's pocket thrust its way into her mind.

"Did you ever discover who the woman in the photograph was?" she asked.

"His mother."

Rupert and Dodo visited Lucille at her hotel and related the whole business. She could not believe it.

"We receive hundreds of unsolicited songs in the mail every year from people hoping Smokey Syncopation will choose theirs. We get so many we hired a secretary to receive all the letters and throw them away. She wouldn't even have told Lonnie about any of them, because she knows we made a deal early on that we would only use our own, original compositions."

"So, Lonnie had no idea who Fred was?" Dodo remarked.

"No, ma'am! None of us knew."

"You can't protect yourself from an unknown enemy," Dodo mused.

Lucille offered her some chocolates. "I'm not such a fan of your English food, but I am totally crazy for your chocolate!"

"I do have one question that never got answered," Dodo said as she selected a noisette crème. "Did Lonnie ever use cocaine? There was some white powder on his trousers when he died."

Lucille clapped her hands together and laughed. "No! Never. I bet it was chalk dust from playing pool. He, Cy and Dex found a pool hall and played earlier that evening to relax before the party. Lonnie was a mean pool player."

Dodo felt the time was right to ask. "When is the cremation?"

Lucille became somber. "Tomorrow at noon. Just the three of us."

"Will you ever come back?"

"You know, when Lonnie was first killed, I was so angry. Angry at England, angry at the world. I thought I'd never come back. But mourning has given me time to change my mind. Heavens to Betsy! The people here have been so gracious, and I love the old buildings, all the history and the mild climate. Lonnie would have loved it. And I want to share our music with the British people. But not yet." She ran a nail over her top lip. "I'm sure we'll have to come over for the trial, but we'll make a real vacation of it. And before that, you will be my guest in New Orleans."

Rupert stared at Dodo wide eyed.

"Oh, yes. I forgot to tell you. I'm going to Lonnie's memorial service. Care to join me?"

"Why not! And I have one more question for Lucille..."

Chapter 24

The music, the flowers, the dress—everything was perfect, but Dodo could not help crying.

Not tears of sorrow, tears of utter joy.

Didi was the most stunning bride she had ever beheld.

Her little sister was getting married!

And since Dodo had known the groom since childhood, she drew comfort from knowing that though he was taking her beloved sister away, he was worthy of her.

Dodo looked over her shoulder at Rupert, who winked, then at her mother, who was dabbing her eyes with a silk handkerchief next to her father, whose chest was puffed so tight she worried his buttons would burst off his waistcoat.

Before she knew it, the vicar was telling the groom to kiss his bride, and Dodo felt the impulse to cheer. Instead, she stepped back to let the newly married couple pass and smiled as the old church bells rang out in celebration, sending their family's joy pulsing through the entire village.

♪

"You look ravishing," said David, who had come to sit at their table after the speeches.

"It's a Renée Dubois," said Dodo simply. "How could I not?" She raised her glass to Renée, who sat on the other side of the white pavilion with her husband. Due to the murder, she and Rupert had not yet gone out to dinner with the couple, but they had plans to in the near future.

In spite of the lavender fabric, Renée had outdone herself on the gown, and Dodo hardly felt like she was wearing anything at all. Though the gown was simple so as not to detract from the splendor of the bride, it felt luxurious and decidedly sexy.

"Who did you come with?" she asked, peering over his shoulder.

"You are not going to believe it," he said quietly. "You are my usual date, and no one else was available."

"Now, I'm really curious," Dodo said.

A peal of laughter came from the back of the tent, and she jerked her eyes to David's. "Not Harriet?"

David looked like a dog who has been caught with a chewed shoe. "Can you believe it? That's how desperate I am without you, darling."

She slapped his shoulder. "It sounds like she said yes to the champagne."

"Great Scott! She's becoming quite the lush. This is absolutely the last time I'm taking her out. I'll probably have to leave early!"

"Poor David. Perhaps she will go straight to the sleepy stage."

"Here's hoping." He gave a little wave as he wandered off to the back of the room.

The exciting thump of smooth jazz traveled across the dance floor and up through the soles of her shoes. As Lucille's velvety voice caressed her skin, Didi and Charlie swayed together in the middle of the dance floor as everyone watched.

"May I have this dance?" asked Rupert after a few minutes from behind her.

Pulling her close, he twirled her around the floor, their bodies in perfect sync with the music.

"Are you happy?" Rupert asked her, running a finger across her collar bone.

"Incandescently," she murmured against his chest.

"That much?" He spoke the words into her hair, sending delectable vibrations through the crown of her head.

From the corner of her eye, she spotted Lizzie and Ernest dancing together, Lizzie in the Dubois gown that Renée had made. Tonight, no one would know she was the

160

maid, as her skin glowed under the loving gaze of her fiancé.

"Then I have my work cut out for me," Rupert said, returning her attention to him.

She pulled away a little and frowned. "Work?"

"I've been trying to think of a way of helping Willie and the other 'lost boys'."

"That is the perfect description! I thought of them as Fagin's crew, but your analogy is better." She tipped her head and his eyes dipped to her lips. "What have you been thinking?"

"A lot of things. A school, a home, a mother figure. But I don't think any of those things will work. They're not fictitious boys in a novel whose wills can be bent to the author's pen. No. They have fashioned a life that works for them outside of the norm because the world failed them."

"Then what?" she asked against his cheek.

"Illiterate men will stay at the bottom echelons of the military. What if I set up a scholarship of some sort that offered them free tutoring when they're older? I think they would appreciate the need to be able to read better then. And it will give them an edge that will help them in their future careers. Teach them to fish, so to speak."

She planted her lips against his. "You marvelous man! That is the perfect solution! We can come up with a special name for it."

"I already did," he said with a grin. "What do you think of *The Artful Dodger Scholarship*?"

She smiled. "Splendid!" After several beats, she continued, "Willie leads a simple life and seems content. Perhaps the rest of us complicate things too much."

"His happiness is relative," said Rupert. "Relative to maltreatment in an orphanage. Relative to starving. His joy would not be ours."

"How wise you are for one so young."

161

Her mother and father sashayed past them. What an anchor for the soul loving parents were.

"You're not the only one who has been thinking about Willie," she said.

"Oh?"

"I'd like to employ him as an investigator from time to time. He can access places where we would stick out like a sore thumb. It would be a way to keep tabs on him without being overbearing."

"The little chap has worked himself into your affections, hasn't he?"

"Guilty!" she declared as Rupert maneuvered her through a clump of couples. "I just had to find a way to help him."

The music stopped, and it was announced that the bride and groom would cut the cake. Didi's eyes were shining as she and Charlie plunged the silver knife into the many-tiered masterpiece.

"You'd look good in white lace," Rupert whispered.

The End

Thanks for buying my book!

Ann Sutton

I hope you enjoyed book 10, *Murder Goes Jazz* and love Dodo as much as I do.

Interested in a **free** prequel to the Dodo Dorchester Mystery series?

Go to https://dl.bookfunnel.com/997vvive24 to download *Mystery at the Derby*.

Book *1* of the series, *Murder at Farrington Hall* is available on Amazon.

https://amzn.to/31WujyS

"Dodo is invited to a weekend party at Farrington Hall. She and her sister are plunged into sleuthing when a murder occurs. Can she solve the crime before Scotland Yard's finest?"

Book 2 of the series, *Murder is Fashionable* is available on Amazon.

https://amzn.to/2HBshwT

"Stylish Dodo Dorchester is a well-known patron of fashion. Hired by the famous Renee Dubois to support her line of French designs, she travels between Paris and London frequently. Arriving for the showing of the Spring 1923 collection, Dodo is thrust into her role as an amateur detective when one of the fashion models is murdered. Working under the radar of the French DCJP Inspector Roget, she follows clues to solve the crime. Will the murderer prove to be the man she has fallen for?"

Book 3 of the series, *Murder at the Races* is available on Amazon.

https://amzn.to/2QIdYKM

*"It is royal race day at Ascot, 1923. Lady Dorothea
Dorchester, Dodo, has been invited by her childhood
friend, Charlie, to an exclusive party in a private box with
the added incentive of meeting the King and Queen.
Charlie appears to be interested in something more than
friendship when a murder interferes with his plans. The
victim is one of the guests from the box and Dodo cannot
resist poking around. When Chief Inspector Blood of
Scotland Yard is assigned to the case, sparks fly between
them again. The chief inspector and Dodo have worked
together on a case before and he welcomes her assistance
with the prickly upper-class suspects. But where does this
leave poor Charlie?
Dodo eagerly works on solving the murder which may have
its roots in the distant past. Can she find the killer before
they strike again?"*

Book 4 of the series, *Murder on the Moors* is available on
Amazon.

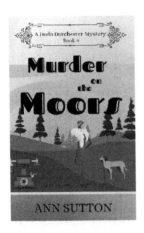

https://amzn.to/38SDX8d

When you just want to run away and nurse your broken heart but murder comes knocking.

"Lady Dorothea Dorchester, Dodo, flees to her cousins' estate in Dartmoor in search of peace and relaxation after her devastating break-up with Charlie and the awkward attraction to Chief Inspector Blood that caused it. Horrified to learn that the arch-nemesis from her schooldays, Veronica Shufflebottom, has been invited, Dodo prepares for disappointment. However, all that pales when one of the guests disappears after a ramble on the foggy moors. Presumed dead, Dodo attempts to contact the local police to report the disappearance only to find that someone has tampered with the ancient phone. The infamous moor fog is too thick for safe travel and the guests are therefore stranded.
Can Dodo solve the case without the help of the police before the fog lifts?"

Book 5 of the series, *Murder in Limehouse* is available on Amazon.

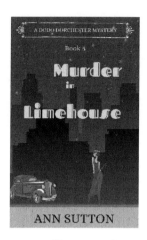

https://amzn.to/3pw2wzQ

Aristocratic star she may be, but when her new love's sister is implicated in a murder, Dodo Dorchester rolls up her designer sleeves and plunges into the slums of London.

Dodo is back from the moors of Devon and diving into fashion business for the House of Dubois with one of the most celebrated department stores in England, while she waits for a call from Rupert Danforth, her newest love interest.

Curiously, the buyer she met with at the store, is murdered that night in the slums of Limehouse. It is only of passing interest because Dodo has no real connection to the crime. Besides, pursuing the promising relationship that began in Devon is a much higher priority.

However, fate has a different plan. Rupert's sister, Beatrice, is arrested for the murder of the very woman Dodo conducted business with at the fashionable store. Now she must solve the crime to protect the man she is fast falling in love with.

Can she do it before Beatrice is sent to trial?

Book *6* of the series, *Murder on Christmas Eve,* is available on Amazon.

https://amzn.to/31VNLyF

Dodo is invited to meet Rupert's family for Christmas. What could possibly go wrong?

Fresh off the trauma of her last case, Dodo is relieved when Rupert suggests spending Christmas with his family at Knightsbrooke Priory.
The week begins with such promise until Rupert's grandmother, Adelaide, dies in the middle of their Christmas Eve dinner. She is ninety-five years old and the whole family considers it an untimely natural death, but something seems off to Dodo who uses the moment of shock to take a quick inventory of the body. Certain clues bring her to draw the conclusion that Adelaide has been murdered, but this news is not taken well.
With multiple family skeletons set rattling in the closets, the festive week of celebrations goes rapidly downhill and

Dodo fears that Rupert's family will not forgive her meddling. Can she solve the case and win back their approval?

Book 7 of the series, *Murder on the Med* is available on Amazon.

https://amzn.to/3PooO99

An idyllic Greek holiday. A murdered ex-pat. Connect the victim to your tourist party, and you have a problem that only Dodo can solve.

Dodo's beau, Rupert, is to meet the Dorchesters for the first time on their annual Greek holiday. He arrives in Athens by train and her family accept him immediately. But rather than be able to enjoy private family time, an eclectic group of English tourists attach themselves to the Dorchesters, and insist on touring the Parthenon with them.

Later that night, a body is found in the very area they had visited and when Dodo realizes that it is the woman she saw earlier, near the hotel, staring at someone in their group, she cannot help but get involved. The over-worked and under-staffed local detective is more than happy for her assistance and between them they unveil all the tourists' dirty secrets.

With help from Rupert and Dodo, can the detective discover the murderer and earn himself a promotion?

Book *8* of the series, *Murder Spoils the Fair* is available on Amazon

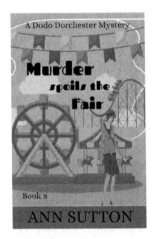

https://amzn.to/42xldFn

A high profile national fair, a murdered model. Can Dodo solve the crime before it closes the fair?

The historic British Empire Fair of 1924 is set to be officially opened by the king at the new Wembley Stadium and Lady Dorothea Dorchester, Dodo, has an invitation.

The whole fair is an attempt to build morale after a devastating World War and the planning and preparation have been in the works for years. So much is riding on its success.

The biggest soap maker in England has been offered the opportunity to host a beauty exhibit and after a nationwide search for the ten most beautiful girls in Britain, they build an extravagant 'palace' that will feature live models representing famous women of history, including one who will represent today's modern woman. Dodo has succeeded in winning the bid to clothe Miss 1924 with fashions from the House of Dubois for whom she is a fashion ambassador.

But the fair has hardly begun when disaster strikes. One of the models is murdered. Can Dodo find the murderer before the bad PR closes the fair?

Book 9 of the series, *Murder Takes a Swing* is available on Amazon

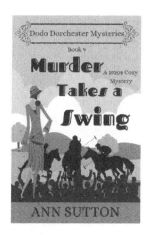

https://amzn.to/3sg3Wn0

High stakes, dark secrets, murder and mayhem. Can Dodo find the killer of Rupert's polo teammate without

endangering their love in the process?

In Murder Takes A Swing, Dodo Dorchester finds herself drawn deep into the glamorous world of polo when one of her beaus' teammates is found murdered the night after their victorious first game of the season.

With the sport of kings as its backdrop, this gripping and unputdownable page-turner will keep you on the edge of your seat as Rupert's friends and teammates become the prime suspects in this deadly game of hidden secrets.

Dodo must use her wits to untangle a web of deceit and betrayal that threatens to unravel everything Rupert thought he knew about his friends. Will she be able to solve the case before the killer strikes again? Can their developing relationship endure the strain?

Full of charm, and suspense, this delightful 1920s cozy mystery will transport you back in time to a world of adventure, and danger, keeping you on the edge of your seat until the very last twist.

Perfect for fans of classic murder mystery novels and historical whodunnits, this is a book you won't want to miss. So, grab your mallet and join the game – the stakes are high and the secrets are deadly.

I am also pleased to announce that I have created a new series, the Percy Pontefract Mysteries. Book *1, Death at a Christmas Party: A 1920's Cozy Mystery,* is available now on Amazon.

https://amzn.to/3Qb4BhG

A merry Christmas party with old friends. A dead body in the kitchen. A reluctant heroine. Sounds like a recipe for a jolly festive murder mystery!

"It is 1928 and a group of old friends gather for their annual Christmas party. The food, drink and goodwill flow, and everyone has a rollicking good time.

When the call of nature forces the accident-prone Percy Pontefract up, in the middle of the night, she realizes she is in need of a little midnight snack and wanders into the kitchen. But she gets more than she bargained for when she trips over a dead body.

Ordered to remain in the house by the grumpy inspector sent to investigate the case, Percy stumbles upon facts about her friends that shake her to the core and cause her to suspect more than one of them of the dastardly deed.

Finally permitted to go home, Percy tells her trusty cook all the awful details. Rather than sympathize, the cook encourages her to do some investigating of her own. After all, who knows these people better than Percy? Reluctant at first, Percy begins poking into her friends' lives, discovering they all harbor dark secrets. However, none seem connected to the murder...at first glance.

Will Percy put herself and her children in danger before she can solve the case that has the police stumped?"

Book *2* of the Percy Pontefract Mysteries, *Death is a Blank Canvasy: A 1920's Cozy Mystery,* is available now on Amazon.

An invitation-only art exhibition. A rising star cut down in his prime. The only suspects, family and a handful of aristocrats. How will Percy navigate these treacherous waters to solve the callous crime?

In this gripping sequel, Percy Pontefract finds herself entangled in a twisted web of murder and lies that strikes painfully close to home, when her talented cousin is brutally killed as the curtain rises on his inaugural modern art exhibition in the heart of London.

The shadow of suspicion looms over everyone present; Percy's colorful relatives and a number of enigmatic aristocrats. When circumstances thrust Percy into detection, she is soon caught up in a dangerous game of cat and mouse as she unravels the truth and concludes that the solution to the murder lies beneath layers of paint, privilege and pretension. She must rely on intuition and luck to avoid becoming the next victim.

Set against a backdrop of the glamorous world of fine art and filled with a cast of eccentric characters, Death Is a Blank Canvas, is a rollicking good whodunnit that will keep you guessing until the very end.

For more information about both series go to my website at www.annsuttonauthor.com and subscribe to my newsletter.

You can also follow me on Facebook at: https://www.facebook.com/annsuttonauthor

About the Author

Agatha Christie plunged me into the fabulous world of reading when I was 10. I was never the same. I read every one of her books I could lay my hands on. Mysteries remain my favorite genre to this day - so it was only natural that I would eventually write my own.

Born and raised in England, writing fiction about my homeland keeps me connected.

After finishing my degree in French and Education and raising my family, writing has become a favorite hobby.

I hope that Dame Agatha would enjoy Dodo Dorchester at much as I do.

Author's note

Once before, I experienced an incredible experience when writing a book that I knew was God telling me I am on the right track. It was book 5. Well, it happened again. I had set this story on the Isle of Dogs. I was almost finished with the rough draft when my husband told me he had been put on a business deal in London. You've guessed it! On the Isle of Dogs. What were the chances? I tagged along and got to do some hands-on research for this book. God is real.

Acknowledgements

I would like to thank all those who have read my books, write reviews and provide suggestions as you continue to inspire.

I would also like to thank my critique partners, Mary Malcarne Thomas and Lisa McKendrick

So many critique groups are overly critical. I have found with you guys a happy medium of encouragement, cheerleading and constructive suggestions. Thank you.

My proof-reader – Tami Stewart

The mothers of a large and growing families who read like the wind with an eagle eye. Thank you for finding little errors that have been missed.

Edited by Waypoint Authors

My cheerleader, marketer and IT guy – Todd Matern

A lot of the time during the marketing side of being an author I am running around with my hair on fire. Todd is the yin to my yang. He calms me down and takes over when I am yelling at the computer.

My beta readers – Francesca Matern, Stina Van Cott,

Your reactions to my characters and plot are invaluable.

The Writing Gals for their FB author community and their YouTube tutorials

These ladies give so much of their time to teaching their Indie author followers how to succeed in this brave new publishing world. Thank you.

Printed in Great Britain
by Amazon

27621108R00106